PENGUIN LIFE

THE BALLERINA MINDSET

Megan Fairchild is a principal dancer with New York City Ballet. After moving from Utah to New York City at the age of sixteen to study ballet full time, she was offered an apprenticeship with NYCB and was promoted to principal—the highest rank—just three years after joining the company. In 2014, she took a temporary leave from NYCB to play the lead role, Miss Turnstiles, in the Broadway musical *On the Town*. She is also the host of the advice podcast *Ask Megan*, a former brand ambassador for Cole Haan, and an MBA student at NYU's Stern School of Business.

THE
BALLERINA
MINDSET

How to Protect Your Mental Health
While Striving for Excellence

Megan Fairchild

life

PENGUIN BOOKS

An imprint of Penguin Random House LLC
penguinrandomhouse.com

A Penguin Life Book

LIBRARY OF CONGRESS CATALOGING-IN-PUBLICATION DATA

Names: Fairchild, Megan, author.
Title: The ballerina mindset : how to protect your mental health while
striving for excellence / Megan Fairchild.
Description: [New York] : Penguin Life, [2021] |
Identifiers: LCCN 2021024500 (print) | LCCN 2021024501 (ebook) |
ISBN 9780525507659 (ebook) | ISBN 9780143136040 (trade paperback) |
Subjects: LCSH: Fairchild, Megan. | Self-actualization (Psychology) |
Success. | Performance. | Stress management. | Work-life balance. |
Life skills. | Ballet dancers—United States—Biography.
Classification: LCC BF637.S4 (ebook) | LCC BF637.S4 F346 2021 (print) |
DDC 158.1—dc23
LC record available at https://lccn.loc.gov/2021024500

Printed in the United States of America
1st Printing

Set in Adobe Garamond Pro
Designed by Cassandra Garruzzo

For my parents,
who gave me every opportunity to succeed
without any pressure

CONTENTS

INTRODUCTION

I started dancing at the age of four and have been deeply immersed in the world of classical ballet since the age of twelve. It is a glamorous, rigorous, and sometimes scandalous world that people like to dramatize in movies and books. In the seventies, ballet culture had an image of being full of sex and drugs, while today, it can sometimes be seen as incredibly sterile, disciplined, and overly intense. It's not for the faint of heart.

Within the industry, there is an immense amount of pressure on young students as they strive toward their dreams of becoming a professional dancer. I remember well how intimidating auditions or competitions can be—how as soon as you arrive you begin to worry about whether you are measuring up to those around you. Young dancers are passionate, but they face a lot of anxiety.

I have spent the last seventeen years as a principal with New York City Ballet, and I can see that the ballet world is mysterious not only to the public but to ballet students, too. When I arrived as a seventeen-year-old apprentice, I was shocked to realize that the exceptional professionals around me were real people, not the perfect beings I had imagined them to be. They ate real food, laughed together, fell down, made mistakes, got back up, and put in the work. Watching people at the height of their artistry and athleticism lead real lives was a revelation for me. We all have doubts, we all have insecurities, and we all wonder if we are good enough—even those at the highest level.

I have always wanted to give back to my community by sharing the lessons I have learned throughout my unique career in a very small and insular field. Because dancers are so human, these are universal insights that can help anyone in any field that they hope to be spectacular in. And because it is through the lens of my time working to be an athlete, artist, and performer, the stories will also give a glimpse into a world often dramatized in the media. I hope to share what it is really like behind the scenes. The highs and lows of working to be your very best. Performing something after hours of hard work with only one or two shows to get it right for an audience of a couple thousand.

All of the lessons I have learned on the way apply to many different paths in life. How do we push ourselves to our limits while holding on to our sanity at the same time? How do we find the balance between striving toward perfection and accepting what we know is our best effort? How do we have full lives while still staying competitive and exceptional in our work? These are the questions that have consumed my mind during my career with NYCB. If you've ever wondered about the answers yourself, then this book is for you, whether you are a dancer, the parent of a dancer, a fan of the ballet, or even someone who has nothing to do with ballet at all.

In these pages I will write about ten crucial lessons I've learned over the course of my career as a ballet dancer and explain how you can use these skills to find your strongest self amid all of life's chaos, stress, and confusion. My hope is that my struggles, fears, and eventual takeaways will help not only younger dancers, but also others who work in completely different industries.

In the last three years, my life has been blessed with three beautiful daughters. I have always felt a responsibility to the young women who are hoping to become professional dancers someday. I want to model proper behavior and especially kindness within a competitive environment. But now I'm also writing this for my own children, in the hopes that they can achieve their dreams with a sense of well-roundedness and balance as well.

THE
BALLERINA
MINDSET

FACING
ANXIETY

❦

How can we deal with
anxiety and stage fright?

In the movie *Black Swan,* the main character, Nina—a young, inexperienced dancer hoping to find success in a big ballet company—suddenly gets cast in the lead role of the company's upcoming production of *Swan Lake.* The movie's portrayal of the moment Nina finds out she has been cast in the role is so accurate, it could have been a scene out of a day in the life of a real ballet company. The casting is announced by a paper posted on the company's bulletin board, and every dancer in the movie strains their neck to see what their part in the production will be. The range of reactions runs the gamut from frustration to contentment to pure exuberance. When Nina sees that she's been cast to dance the coveted lead role of the Swan Queen, her first response isn't one of pure excitement and celebration. Instead, in a state of shock, she goes into a bathroom stall to cry. What she thought she wanted, or secretly hoped for deep down, is now terrifying as she thinks about the pressure and responsibility—not only of dancing the lead without much prior experience, but also of doing it while other dancers breathe down her neck with jealousy. When I saw the movie, this scene resonated with me so much, because it mirrored the fear and dread I felt when I was given my first opportunities as a professional dancer.

In November of 2001, at the age of seventeen, I was offered an apprenticeship with New York City Ballet. Ever since our School of American Ballet workshop performance the previous June, my classmates and I had been in the dark about whether the company was interested in hiring us. Waiting for that first job offer is a strange time for a dancer. In fact, I almost took a position with San Francisco Ballet that summer instead. But I made one last effort to come back to SAB and try my luck at NYCB—and fortunately, it worked out. When the director of NYCB, Peter Martins, finally called me and nine of my friends into the office at SAB, I was beyond thrilled . . . and relieved!

The very next year, I began getting a couple of soloist and principal parts, even though I was only a corps member. My very first soloist role that year—a pas de deux in Balanchine's *Chaconne*—was a perfect first role in the spotlight, because it was short and sweet, and very well suited to my style of dancing. However, I was completely unprepared mentally to deal with the stress of a featured role. I stayed up until four in the morning before that performance, unable to sleep, crying on the phone to my mom in

Utah that I would not be able to perform well in the show because I didn't yet feel like I was performing consistently in my rehearsals. I was also dealing with a lot of back pain from trying to do certain steps, and I later found out that I had three vertebrae twisted in opposite directions, which was completely limiting my mobility. Back pain, I would come to discover, can go hand in hand with emotional stress, and it is no surprise that the anxiety I felt in this first show manifested itself in my body.

Thankfully, the show went well, despite my exhaustion from stressing the entire night before, and my superiors were happy. Each opportunity in our company is like a little test, and if you pass each one to the boss's satisfaction, you are given a new challenge. I later came to think of company life as one big season of the reality show *Survivor*.

One thing led to another, and I began to learn principal roles here and there. Each of those opportunities came with only one or two weeks' notice before the actual performance date, so it was all a whirlwind. I always had so much anxiety and stress built up in my body before each debut performance, although it was never as bad as that first night. When the performances finished, crying for a while was the only way to release all that adrenaline. They weren't even sad tears—they were just a way to vent the stress and pressure I had accumulated in accomplishing each task. It scared me at first, letting off built-up stress like this, but I began to accept it as the way my body was processing all the pressure. As time went on, it scared me less and less—this life was becoming my new normal.

By the summer of my second year in the corps, I had the opportunity to understudy the lead role in my first full-length ballet, *Coppélia*. I was able to prepare with relatively little pressure, as there were at least three principal ballerinas ready to do the four shows in Saratoga Springs, where NYCB performs every summer. It seemed like an honor just to be learning the ballet.

But upon arriving in Saratoga, I was called to meet with the head of our corps de ballet. She informed me that all three principal ballerinas were injured and I would be performing all four *Coppélia* performances by myself. Two of them would even occur in the same day—a matinee followed by an evening performance. I would be dancing with two principal men, Damian Woetzel and Benjamin Millepied, both exceptional and legendary dancers whom I had always admired from afar.

I remember staying polite and professional in front of the ballet mistress who gave me this shocking news, but as soon as I turned around to walk back to my dressing room, my eyes flooded with tears of overwhelming fear. How would this even be possible? I didn't even know if I could do one full-length *Coppélia*, let alone all four, and two of them in the same day with no recovery time at all! Just like Nina in *Black Swan*, I was overwhelmed by the responsibility of my director's choices and trust in me, and I just wanted to run away and hide.

In that next week leading up to the shows, I clung to the trust and confidence that I felt my director had put in me. There wasn't a ton of nit-picking and adjusting my dancing in rehearsals—there wasn't any time. I found out many years later that some of the other ballet masters thought it impossible, or crazy, that I was asked to accomplish such a task. This is one of those situations in which ignorance was bliss! If I had heard that anyone else thought it was insane, just like I believed deep down it was, I would never have been able to accomplish the task confidently.

In the end, the performances went miraculously well. Once a performance had begun, I felt much less nervous than I had in the days leading up to it. In a full-length ballet, you have entrance after entrance, which is basically opportunity after opportunity to redeem yourself if something previously didn't go well. I also had some kind senior corps members helping me with little positive mantras and offering advice. One told me, "Carb up before the show, and eat lots of protein afterward to repair the muscles." Another let me borrow her dressing room Wonder Woman Barbie doll, which came along with the mantra, "I am Diva Bitch, I will rock." Looking back, that sounds hysterical, but in the moment you take what you can get and hold on to anything that seems positive and inspiring! One of the principal dancers watching a rehearsal told me that I had good instincts and to trust myself. Knowing that a couple of older dancers believed in me really helped me go out there and dance my best.

To make up for my lack of confidence during my early years as a principal, I often just pretended to be the ballerinas I admired. It made me feel safer onstage to pretend to be a principal who already had all the experience and confidence she needed, and who had spent years developing her technique and artistry for that particular ballet. When you're just starting out, I think it's okay to trick yourself this way if it helps you feel more confident.

> *To make up for my lack of confidence during my early years as a principal, I often just pretended to be the ballerinas I admired. . . . When you're just starting out, I think it's okay to trick yourself this way if it helps you feel more confident.*

Coppélia showcased my best traits as a dancer, and I was dancing with two incredibly experienced and helpful partners. However, I soon learned that one success was not enough for me to conquer my anxiety. I needed time, experience, and more coping mechanisms before I could trust in my abilities. This became obvious the next season.

That fall, a twenty-seven-year-old Spaniard from American

Ballet Theatre, Joaquín De Luz, joined our company. He was incredibly talented but on the shorter side, just five foot six, and needed a smaller girl to be partnered with. Because I was also on the shorter side, at five foot three and a half, the company thought to partner us for his first try at the Sugar Plum pas de deux in the *Nutcracker*. Of course it's an honor to see your name on the schedule to learn a big new part like that, and at first I felt so much excitement and joy. But then the doom of the responsibility and the horrible gloom of doubt started to settle in—again just like Nina in *Black Swan*. An opportunity that seemed like what every dancer would hope for hung on my shoulders like a heavy weight pulling me down, making every day seem exhausting and difficult.

Joaquín and I struggled at first. He was adjusting to the difference between the ABT style of partnering and our style at NYCB, which is to be much farther away from your partner. It was terrifying—in certain positions, I felt like I was teetering on the edge of a cliff. I would ultimately fall off pointe and we would have to try again. We must have rehearsed certain steps in that pas de deux a hundred times that November. I felt horrible for the pianist, who kept having to repeat the same four bars of music for us. It was demoralizing to have to keep trying over and over. I remember watching experienced principals Maria Kowroski and Charles Askegard rehearse in front of the whole company for the opening night of *Nutcracker* that year, and I just couldn't believe how easy they made it look.

All of the rehearsals started to take a toll on my body, and I strained my inner thigh the week before our first scheduled show. I was taken out of my corps parts and rehearsals to rest and made it back to the stage just in time for our first performance, feeling even less confident than before.

The day of the show arrived, and as "Waltz of the Flowers" finished and the corps dancers bowed and ran off, I saw the lighting change that signaled our entrance. I started to get nervous. The lighting for the pas has a beautiful romantic feel to it—they dim from the bright lights of the "Waltz of the Flowers," and as Sugar Plum enters, two huge spotlights catch her and her partner and stay with them for the entire five minutes. I vividly remember that as I took my first steps out into those stark bright spotlights, my immediate thought was, "I want to run back into the wings." I wasn't comfortable in the lighting, I wasn't comfortable having all of my colleagues watching from the wings in expectation, and I desperately wanted to stop and say, "Just a minute!" but I couldn't. The orchestra played on.

Joaquín had such a confident posture, and it reminded me that I couldn't express my anxiety. This is what makes dance so difficult—we aren't allowed to show the effort, fear, or exhaustion that comes into play during a performance. We become experts in keeping ourselves pulled together and making everything look confident and effortless when sometimes we feel the opposite inside. I pushed my shoulders down, put a smile on my face, and tried to pretend everything was fine, when inside I wanted to curl up in a ball and cry or scream or just simply run away.

We got to the very first step of the pas de deux and something felt funny in our spacing. I fell off pointe. I tried to brush it off and move onto the next step, but felt uncomfortable again, and fell off pointe. Nothing was going right. It was as if we were an ice-skating couple falling after each jump attempt.

The middle part of the pas is a blur. My body was in shock from the beginning having been such a failure. When I got to the famous moment toward the end where I am supposed to appear to slide in arabesque as he pulls me with one hand across the stage, I failed to properly step on the slide mechanism on the floor. As I went up into the position, my body swung around and Joaquín couldn't figure out how to help me. So I stepped off the slide and just did a piqué arabesque.

After the performance my brother and dad came backstage. I burst into tears when I saw them. I was so disappointed in myself. All of those weeks of rehearsal, figuring out how to accomplish the role for our bodies and heights, and learning to work together—all for such a terrible result. My perfectionist mentality couldn't handle it. My dad just smiled and hugged me. He was used to me never being satisfied. But I felt truly frustrated as that was definitely one of our worst run-throughs.

My boss and ballet master were not as hard on me as I was on myself (a theme throughout my life and career), but I couldn't recover from the epic failure of that performance. We went on to do one other performance that season. I know that one was much better, but I don't have any recollection of that performance. I only remember the one that felt like a failure.

WE'VE ALL EXPERIENCED THOSE MOMENTS when our breathing stops, our reasoning and perspective grow clouded, and doubt sets in. Suddenly, we have no faith in our ability to accomplish the task before us. Welcome to the world of anxiety.

Anxiety's many manifestations seem endless. For some people, public speaking brings on severe anxiety. For others, getting on an airplane triggers it. Sometimes the reason for it is understandable, like going to a job interview or starting a new job. And other times it is completely ridiculous, like the fear of getting locked in a bathroom. (I will admit to this very absurd, but very real, anxiety. Every time I use a public restroom, I rush to finish so I can unlock the door, as I have no faith that the lock will release and let me out.)

Anxiety can be caused by a few different kinds of fear. First, there's fear of failure—doubting your ability to execute something properly, whether it's not making a deadline, being late, not meeting people's expectations, or not being able to fulfill your responsibilities, be it at work or at home. For me it was the fear of dancing poorly in front of an audience of two-thousand-plus people when I didn't know my strengths.

Second, there's fear of the unknown—the fear that things

might happen to you that you don't have control over, like loved ones getting sick or injured, or not fitting into a group. Or a live performance when no matter how prepared and capable you might be, anything is possible: costume malfunction, a shoe becoming untied, a headpiece falling off, dropping a prop, forgetting the choreography . . . the unknown is endless in the world of live performing.

Then there is the worst of them all: the fear of having fear. It's the PTSD of anxiety. Whenever we've doubted our ability to handle a situation, the next time that situation crops up, we might worry that all those fears will come back to haunt us and weigh us down again. It's worrying that we'll be worried. Fearing that we will fear. It's the worst anxiety of them all because it can become a vicious cycle.

Throughout my career, ballets that had caused me a lot of stress in my debuts continued to make me nervous the next time they came around. Sometimes they caused anxiety because they were just so difficult and it was hard to be consistent in my execution. Others could make me nervous because they were just so physically exhausting, stamina-wise, and I feared the exhaustion that I knew would be coming my way.

This anxiety still manifests in the week or two leading up to an important show for me. My stomach suddenly feels funny and I get a bit on edge in all areas of life. I often don't recognize the true source of these symptoms until they all disappear at the same time when that scary show is over and has gone well. It is only then that

I realize the power anxiety can have on your body physically and mentally.

So we have fear of failure, fear of the unknown, and fear of having fear. But couldn't we just find one common thread connecting all three? Anxiety is fearing the outcome of something. We have written out a script of the worst possible scenario in our heads, and we spend all of our time and energy obsessing that it may come true.

When you put it that way, you realize how ridiculous any worry truly is. No matter how advanced our society becomes, we will never be able to predict the future. This means that worrying about an outcome, when you truly have no idea how you will perform in a given situation or how something will pan out, is a waste of energy. Why are we assuming the worst before the event has even happened? What's more, you start to see how distracting that focus is. Instead of worrying about the possibility of failure, you could be focusing on setting yourself up to prepare for the best possible result.

By worrying, we think we are more actively controlling a situation, but it's a false sense of security. It gives our anxious minds something to do—something that feels productive but in reality is hindering us from being able to create a successful outcome. It is like that first show of *Chaconne*, when I stayed up until four in the morning allowing those worst-case scenarios to play out in my head, when I should have been sleeping and resting my body so that I would be physically ready for the demands of the next day. We waste so much time and energy on being worried—time and energy that would be better spent preparing ourselves for the big moment.

> *By worrying, we think we are more actively controlling a situation, but it's a false sense of security. It gives our anxious minds something to do—something that feels productive but in reality is hindering us from being able to create a successful outcome.*

I think this tendency is common for people who put a lot of pressure on themselves to be perfect and leave no room for mistakes or a learning curve. Right off the bat, we have decided to doubt ourselves. What a shame, too, because life is hard enough even if we aren't on our own side. We need to give ourselves our best opportunity to succeed, and it starts with being our own advocate for our greatest possible potential.

You might find that your current coping mechanisms for anxiety fall into one of two categories: complete avoidance and denial, or else a severe emotional response. How many of you have been so frozen with fear about a project that you can't even begin to work on it? Or maybe you deal with your fear much more emotionally, with a torrential downpour of tears. Both are ways we naturally process fear and anxiety, but they are not helpful. They are self-saboteurs masked as safety blankets.

We can't always control the amount of stress or pressure in our lives, but we can learn to develop coping mechanisms so that we no longer sabotage the outcome. Finally, after many years as a professional dancer, I was able to develop some of my own strategies to control my anxiety.

As TIME PASSED, Joaquín and I continued to dance the *Nutcracker* pas together, slowly growing in the role. We became really consistent in our performances and learned ways to approach the steps so they worked for us. These weren't things that a ballet master could have necessarily taught us. All they really could do was teach us the steps, tell us what our dancing looked like, and give us their support. We were the only ones feeling the steps for ourselves, and had to be the ones to discover the tricks and tools we needed. I was the only one in my body knowing if I felt on balance or not, and the only way I figured that out was by performing and practicing. I came to trust the stage as my ultimate teacher, telling me in the moment where my balance needed to be to make the step happen live in front of each audience. I was beginning to learn that giving in to my anxiety and believing I could fail—in fact, meditating on that—was no way to succeed. I had to put all of my energy and focus into positive actions like rehearsing well, getting sleep, eating right—taking care of me. The things I could control.

Eleven years after that first failed performance, my boss stopped me in the hallway to let me know he would unfortunately not be able to let Joaquín and me dance any outside gigs that *Nutcracker* season. (A perk of being a principal is that at *Nutcracker* time we are allowed to take on outside work to earn extra money performing with other schools or smaller companies in the lead roles of their *Nutcracker*s.) I was bummed, but politely told him I would do whatever the company needed. And then he told me why. Our company would be filming *Nutcracker* live for PBS one night, and again a second night to be telecast in movie theaters around the world, and he wanted Joaquín and me to do the pas.

Again, excitement set in at first, followed by horrible dread. We had become quite consistent in the pas de deux, having performed it together for a decade by then, but to expect ourselves to be able to perform well under the pressure of live cameras capturing our every move was just like being nineteen again, stunned by those spotlights. I felt like it was my debut in the role all over again.

Leading up to the show, I knew it wouldn't be enough to just prepare my body physically. This was an opportunity that wouldn't allow for mistakes or second tries, and I had to find a way to make sure my mental game was as strong as my physical one. There would be no time for the moment to be clouded by anxiety, and I had to find a way to deal with it, once and for all. I came to terms with the realization that anxiety never goes away, even as a seasoned professional. Instead I had to learn to redirect that energy toward more positive aspects of the experience that I was able to control.

> *I came to terms with the realization that anxiety never goes away, even as a seasoned professional. Instead I had to learn to redirect that energy toward more positive aspects of the experience that I was able to control.*

Searching for books that might help me deal with stress in the self-help section of the bookstore, I found a book about imagery and meditation called *Life Shift: Let Go and Live Your Dream*, by Aleta St. James. I didn't necessarily know whether it would help me, but I was in a try-anything-and-everything kind of place—that very open and willing attitude that comes from being completely vulnerable in a situation and knowing you need some outside help.

The book spoke right to my issues, teaching me how to stay grounded and develop a stronger and more resilient mental capacity for the stress. I took a lot of the meditation baths she recommended and imagined orbs of light of specific colors coming into my body through the top of my head. Sometimes I would look at myself and think, "Jeez, you are really losing it, girl," but embracing these techniques of imagery to calm my overly active anxiety became a way to survive. Energy and imagery work are great tools if you believe in their transformative power, and I was ready to embrace anything to help me feel more stable.

According to St. James, when we feel a strong emotion, our first reaction is usually to panic, which causes our breathing to become shallower and keeps us from processing these important emotions. By utilizing imagery and different deep breathing techniques, we can keep ourselves from suppressing emotions and successfully move on from them instead. Different colors relate to different emotions: envisioning a bright orange sun and its rays beating down on you helps you process anger; cobalt blue helps with feelings of confusion; and pink helps for sadness. The idea is to breathe in the color for your specific negative emotion, ask yourself what fear is hiding behind it, and let the color dissolve your anger, confusion, or sadness until you feel a sense of peace.

Embracing these techniques of imagery to calm my overly active anxiety became a way to survive.

The day of the first performance, I got ready ahead of time and went backstage to watch the earlier parts of the ballet. I had my headphones on to stay grounded and was listening to classic rock, a genre I grew up loving because of my dad's influence. It always made me feel safe and at home. I tried to just enjoy the moment. The company looked so good, and I was so proud to be part of this special moment.

The second act arrived quickly, and as we approached the pas, I automatically went into a "don't think about what's happening" mentality. I couldn't allow myself to realize that the performance I had prepared for so many months was finally here. Letting thoughts like "Oh, here is the step that tripped you up in rehearsal a week ago," or "Here is a step that people might be judging closely" process through me would have made me shaky and nervous as I tried to cope with the pressure of a performance that was being filmed live and would live on forever.

As soon as we walked out on stage, I knew my brain needed something comforting and familiar to focus on so I could stay steady in my legs. While warming up, I had listened to the song "Hotel California" by the Eagles, and as I stepped out onto the stage, I started singing the lyrics in my head. I kept it up through the entire pas de deux, singing in time with the music coming from the orchestra pit. It helped me create a calmer experience for myself inside my brain. If I had turned off my internal classic rock station, I would have thought about what I was doing in that moment, and my body would have tensed up and become shaky.

This survival tactic wasn't anything I had read about or planned to do. It just occurred to me in the moment. I felt my mind want to panic and I needed to find an immediate landing point for it, and so I used the last song I had been listening to in order to keep me grounded and out of my head.

I knew my brain needed something comforting and familiar to focus on so I could stay steady in my legs . . . and as I stepped out onto the stage, I started singing the lyrics in my head. . . . It helped me create a calmer experience for myself inside my brain.

It worked. We executed the pas perfectly. I had never felt so proud of something I had done as I was at that moment in my career. Whatever else happened, I felt like I could hang my hat on those two successful live performances. I had filmed an iconic role, a role that every young dancer knows, in a way that immortalized Joaquín and myself.

I KNOW I WILL never stop feeling fear or doubt, but with years of experience, I've learned how to leave the limiting emotions backstage so that I can function my best during performances. When

I think back to my first experience with that *Nutcracker* pas, and then look to where I was able to get to mentally, as well as physically, it's hard to believe the difference. To go from a place of such doubt and fear to completely owning the moment and powering through is still unbelievable to me today.

What I carry most from that opportunity is the realization that you can't rush experience. And experience is what builds consistency. And consistency yields confidence.

When you start any project that seems impossible, your experience—and in turn, your confidence—is starting out at its lowest level. But no one has to know that you don't quite trust yourself yet. In fact, they are probably leaving space for the fact that you will be making mistakes. It is important to take the process step-by-step and not expect to be perfect right out of the gate.

The more something matters to us—whether it is to perform a ballet, run a marathon, go on a blind date, or go to that big job interview—the worse our anxiety about it becomes. But the anxiety lives in the anticipation. Not in the actual event.

Learn not to write the story beforehand. Let it play out without judging how you are worried it will be. The stress you let in will take away energy you need for the actual event. Say no to your former coping mechanisms that are only self-sabotaging, and yes to new ones that help you trust yourself. And remember, even your anxiety's worst-case scenario—failure—isn't always permanent. Life is more forgiving than that, and more times than not, we have second chances.

EMBRACING
UNIQUENESS

*How can we stop worrying
about our "flaws"?*

Growing up, I was always the shortest girl in my dance class. It was easy for my parents to spot me in our performances: I was the little one. In part the height discrepancy was because I was often in classes with people a little bit older than me, but in general, at five foot three and a half, I have always been more petite than average.

The advantage of being short was that I never had a growth spurt, which was probably beneficial to my dance training as I never suddenly found myself with a lot of new height that I had to learn how to coordinate. But the downside is that ballet is a visual art form and the look of a group of dancers from afar is part of the picture, so it's important for dancers to fit in with one another. Also, when you're a taller solo dancer, the audience can see you better from afar, and you can cover greater space onstage, which is more exciting from the audience's perspective.

As I got older, my mom and I began to wonder if there was a

place in the ballet world for someone as petite as me. The professional company in Utah had extreme height requirements—at the time, women had to be five foot six or taller to audition and men had to be six feet or taller. Not knowing much about the industry outside of Utah, my mom and I were concerned that my height might get in the way of any possible career.

I will never forget the first phone conversation I had with my mom after going to New York to attend the SAB's six-week summer intensive. Right away, she asked, "Are you the shortest?"

I told my mom I was one of the shorter girls, but I definitely wasn't the shortest. I was so worried about looking different, and just wanted to blend in.

My first year in the company, I realized I was the second-shortest dancer in the entire group of one hundred or so company members. The one girl shorter than me was five foot two, and the tallest girl in the company was around five foot ten, so I was very much at that low end of the spectrum. By this point, though, I didn't care. They had already accepted me. I was just happy I had enough of the right look to make it into the company.

What is nice about NYCB is that they allow a range of body types. Most American companies are this way, but if you look at international companies like Paris Opera or the Bolshoi, everyone has to fit into a more specific mold. The dancers have to have the right height, the right foot, the right leg line, the right proportions. At NYCB those things are important, but there is more leeway. You will see in American companies a much wider variety of heights, proportions, and musculature.

My height definitely affected my company schedule in a negative way at the beginning. I wasn't picked to understudy standard large corps ballets like *Serenade* or *Stars and Stripes* like my fellow apprentices. I didn't really mind—I was busy enough, and I was happy to ease into the adjustment to company life.

Little did I know this slow adjustment would only last for a couple of months, because I was soon picked for small soloist and principal roles here and there. Maybe it was because my height helped me to stand out that I got attention, but whatever the case, those first few roles, while incredibly scary, made up for the fact that I didn't get to participate in the bigger ballets like everyone else. While it was hard to be on a different path than my colleagues, and I would have truly enjoyed the bonding experience of being in those big corps ballets, I realized I was on my own special journey, so I embraced what life brought me.

Two years after I joined the company as an apprentice it was announced that two new men from other companies would be joining our ranks. (This is a very rare occurrence at NYCB, where usually the only way to get into the company is by attending SAB in your teen years. However, male talent can be hard to come by in the ballet world, and if the company connects with a talented male dancer who has always had a dream of dancing in Balanchine's company, then they may relax the rules. This is just something you accept in the industry—that the competition among women is much more intense and unforgiving than it is for men.) One of the dancers was Ask la Cour, a towering six-foot, three-inch Dane who would be joining us from the Royal Danish Ballet as a corps member. The other new member was a five-foot, six-inch soloist from ABT named . . . you guessed it, Joaquín De Luz.

I didn't think much of it when Joaquín entered the company that fall for his first tour with us in Copenhagen. But just a month later, we were already paired together for that first *Nutcracker*—the inexperienced nineteen-year-old with the seasoned twenty-seven-year-old. Despite what I thought was a completely failed first performance together, we apparently complemented each other very well visually onstage, and from that moment on we were each other's go-to partner. My short stature, which had prevented me from even auditioning for other companies, had made me the perfect partner for Joaquín.

A few months later, I was called into my boss's office with two other dancers and was promoted to soloist. It was a shock, because dancers usually stay in the corps for four or more years, and I had only been a corps member for one and a half. Being promoted was not even on my radar. I felt like I had just arrived and was still proving myself in my new roles on stage. I had so much still to learn. Yet it was exciting news to be promoted to soloist, and I remember having extra jitters the next day while performing, with my new title and the expectations that I felt went along with it.

The next January I got called into Peter's office again, this time with Joaquín. I knew this one wouldn't be as happy a meeting as the last one was. The month prior, I had accidentally left a tutu rental from the company on an airplane when returning home from a *Nutcracker* gig with Joaquín. The flight attendant thought it would be safer to hang my tutu in the coat closet at the front of the plane, and when we deboarded I completely forgot to grab it. Tutus cost anywhere from five thousand to ten thousand dollars, so this was not only an embarrassing mistake but also an expensive one. I realized that five thousand dollars would need to come out of my paycheck to pay for this moment of absentmindedness.

"I hear there is a missing tutu," Peter began. I started to explain what had happened. Halfway into my story, I saw the main ballet mistress, who was also in the meeting, and Peter start to smile. Then Peter said, "That's not really why you are here! You are being promoted!"

My jaw dropped. The whole tutu affair had completely thrown me off guard, but on top of that, I had only been a soloist for less than a year. This was news I just could not comprehend. I remember I kept repeating, "Are you sure? Is this real? Are you sure?" It made sense for Joaquín to get promoted, with his level of experience, but I felt sure my own promotion was a mistake. We walked down the hallway from the offices together with completely different reactions: one of us fulfilled and content, the other in a complete state of shock and confusion. I was actually still wondering about how they were going to reprimand me for the tutu. (In the end, they casually put the tutu story to bed. They never brought it up again, and I was never docked pay for the missing costume. A promotion and a get out of jail free card!)

Joaquín and I went on to share the next fourteen years of our careers together. We danced with other partners, but if we were both learning a ballet, the staff cast us as a couple. I learned to embrace my height not as my weakness, but as my advantage. If I had been three inches taller at five foot six, a height that I think would be ideal as a dancer, I would never have had the opportunities that ended up coming my way. The most unique thing about me—the thing that made me stand out, the thing I was always a bit embarrassed about—ended up being my ticket to the front of the line.

The most unique thing about me—the thing that made me stand out, the thing I was always a bit embarrassed about—ended up being my ticket to the front of the line.

In a company as large as NYCB, there are enough dancers so that each role can be given to the dancer who is perfectly suited to it. The roles that have quick footwork or lots of jumps and turns are usually given to the shorter dancers. And beautiful adagios are saved for the taller dancers. So when my boss took me aside during a *Nutcracker* intermission one night to ask me how I felt about doing *Swan Lake*, you can imagine my surprise.

Swan Lake was always for the tall ballerinas. It wasn't something I had ever set my mind on. My very first ballet teacher from Utah would always ask me when I would get the opportunity to perform this ballet, and I would have to explain that *Swan Lake* is for the tall dancers. I didn't mind. I felt that I already had plenty of challenging ballets to sink my teeth into, and most of all, I liked doing what I was suited for. I had no interest in being pushed to do something that would not put me in my best light.

In fact, when Peter asked me about *Swan Lake*, I thought maybe he meant just the Balanchine version, which is only the second act. Surely he couldn't mean the entire full-length ballet. I think I responded, "What do you mean? Which part of *Swan Lake*?"—probably not the answer he expected. I had never even entertained the idea of seeing myself in this role. But he thought it would be fun and that it was time. I was thirty-three years old for my debut.

I don't know if I was the shortest person to ever dance this ballet with NYCB, but I was definitely one of the shortest. It was usually reserved for dancers like Maria Kowroski or Sara Mearns, and I never shared any roles with those dancers. Working to make up for the difference in height was going to take a lot of thought, preparation, and coaching. I was really worried that I wouldn't be able to sell myself as a long swan given my short frame.

I started focusing on my Gyrotonic training to make my

shoulders more flexible for all of the beautiful port de bras required. I also got a Russian coach who used to teach at SAB, Olga Kostritzky, to work with me before rehearsal period with the company even started. She is a master at teaching classical roles and helped me understand the passion and the beauty that you need to express in a role of this magnitude. I focused on the ways I could achieve the same positions as these taller dancers, making sure I made the most out of the lines that I did have. I was growing as an artist. To have tackled a ballet that in my mind was the pinnacle of a tall dancer's career was rewarding and gave me great satisfaction. It took me a long time to believe that I was worthy of a role like that.

It was a wonderful lesson in the beauty of uniqueness. Every dancer who has ever graced the stage is different from the one before. We spend a lot of our time in society trying to fit in and embrace trends. But it would be one boring world if in fact we did all look and act the same. We need to learn to discover, and then embrace, what sets us apart. It may be what gets us noticed, even if we think it's a "flaw"—and what gives us that crucial first opportunity.

Maybe your uniqueness is something that is really hard to imagine as anything but a weakness. Perhaps you are a slow learner, or have trouble focusing at work. However, if you struggle with something, you will have to work that much harder to accomplish what might come easily for others. And that effort and drive you have to put into it will make you a more resilient and determined worker, who may possibly go on to surpass your peers. This is often true in ballet, where dancers with many natural gifts and talents can become complacent and start to plateau.

Uniqueness does not equal weakness, unless you allow it to mentally hold you back. Turn that difference into your strength, and make it your ticket to the top. How can it shape and mold you into becoming the best version of yourself?

As a shorter dancer there are lots of steps that were incredibly easy for me, such as petit allegro or any kind of quick footwork. Even turns and jumps can be easier as there is less length to coordinate for each movement. I learned to work even harder on those steps so that I could become the clear go-to dancer for ballets involving lots of them. Of course, I tried to improve all aspects of my dancing, but I also made sure to capitalize on the strengths that came from my height.

It's funny looking back now and remembering how much my mom and I were worried about my height in the ballet world. In the end, it was my secret weapon to initially get noticed. We all stand out from the crowd in some way, and usually, we make ourselves feel bad about not fitting in. But if we remember to embrace our uniqueness, we can use it to our benefit. As a bonus, the confidence that comes from owning ourselves, strengths and weaknesses alike, is an attractive thing. People will be drawn to that.

Don't let your differences hold you back . . . make them work for you!

BALANCING
THE SCALE

*How can we come to terms
with the sacrifices we have
to make in order to achieve
our goals?*

Growing up, I didn't think about weight until I came back from my first summer course at SAB. After five weeks of intense dancing, I had somehow gained several pounds. It had been my first time eating on my own, and the cafeteria at the ballet school was filled with things that my family never kept in our house. Having a mother who was a dietitian meant that we didn't keep junk food around. The SAB cafeteria, on the other hand, was like one big fun pantry. I didn't go crazy, but I definitely ate things I didn't usually eat.

After the shocking realization that I had gained weight, too rapidly for it to have been a growth spurt, my mom taught me the sobering details of what a calorie is. It was the most depressing conversation. I spent the next hour sadly snacking on carrots and realizing life was suddenly a bit less fun. I mean, it is a sad moment when you realize that there are healthy and unhealthy food choices to make, and that all the fun things are unhealthy! I remember the jugs of frothy OJ I used to drink from concentrate that accompanied my huge waffle or stack of pancakes on Saturday mornings as a kid. Suddenly learning that the number of calories in those fun-filled, carefree childhood mornings was close to the number of calories one needed in a whole day made me sad. It was like the end of my innocence in a way. The end of a dancer's childhood.

Like every other member of my family, I have a healthy appetite and really enjoy a good meal. During the school year after that first summer at SAB, I was constantly starving because I was dancing so much. Only two hours after breakfast I would already be eating a Clif Bar and some string cheese. At lunchtime I would grab a slice of pepperoni cheese pizza and a huge sugar cookie with frosting. We never kept cookies or sweets at home, so I ate one at school every day. During the drive from school to ballet, I would snack on one of those little packs of fake cheese with the sticks to dip in it, or some corn nuts—or whatever my mom had grabbed for me. Dinner was a well-rounded and healthy meal my parents made, always consisting of a veggie, meat, and starch. I may have known how many calories were in everything, but it didn't change my eating habits that much.

By my second summer at SAB, my body had filled out, and a gay friend from the year before commented on my new womanly figure. Now that my friends had seen my body change from one year to the next, I became a little more self-conscious. My hormones had started to do their own thing.

The next year, I made the big decision to train full-time at SAB and moved from my parents' home in Utah to the SAB dorm on Manhattan's Upper West Side. I was very busy every day with high school, two ballet classes, and sometimes extra rehearsals. My schedule kept me in shape, no matter what weird stuff I happened to grab from the cafeteria. I remember some other dancers freaking out about their weight, especially before our spring workshop performance, which put the "issue of weight" back on my radar. But I still didn't do anything differently. I was just becoming aware.

The following year I joined the company as an apprentice. I had an incredible sweet tooth and no one to tell me, "Don't spoil your dinner." They used to sell these homemade cookies in the dorm cafeteria. There was nothing special about them, but they were my guilty pleasure. Every day after my first ballet class, before heading back to the high school, I used to make a "lunch" that consisted of two packets of oatmeal with a banana and three of the cookies. It completely satisfied my sweet tooth, and hey, I was eating a banana! Friends around me were having salads or sandwiches, and I had managed this sneaky trick of making lunch a dessert.

Cafeteria-style eating in a ballet dorm is very socially complex. There were girls who wouldn't eat in front of anyone, taking their salads in brown bags up to their rooms, with one whole-wheat roll that they would slather in zero-calorie I Can't Believe It's Not Butter! spray. (Side note: Per serving that spray has no calories, but a dietitian I know once sent it in for testing. A container of it has about nine hundred calories! What messed-up advertising!!!) On weekends, those same girls would binge-eat at the dorm movie night, which included dorm-provided snacks like boxes of Entenmann's goodies, cheese, candy, and other guilty pleasures. Looking back, I'm sure the dorm staff meant well, but this was doing nothing to help us with balance. The message being sent seemed to be: "Be a perfect ballerina and eat perfectly all week, and then you can be a normal junk food kid on the weekends." But when you are restricting your diet like a lot of the dancers around me were, being exposed to a table full of treats is just a binge session waiting to happen. I wasn't yet very messed up mentally with my eating, but I did watch other girls who had been eating salads all week stuff their faces until they were literally hugging the toilet bowl from feeling so sick.

There were other girls who would only eat frozen yogurt for a meal. There was this place on Seventy-second Street that advertised yogurt with only eight calories per serving, aptly called Only 8. I often enjoyed a small cup, at one point even once a day, but I saw other girls take a literal pint back home and eat it as their only thing for dinner.

I remember one Saturday afternoon when I was super hungry and went down to the cafeteria to grab a slice of cheesecake and one of those bags of three soft cookies. Feeling a little gluttonous, I got into the elevator to go back up to the dorms. Right before the doors closed, the director of our school entered the elevator. I tried to smile like there was nothing wrong with holding a pile of sweets in my arms. She didn't act like anything was amiss, but I was humiliated. It felt weird for a teacher to see my eating habits, and even weirder for her to see a particularly bad moment. I wondered what she was thinking about me. Did she think that I wasn't taking care of myself? Did I look like a dancer who wasn't taking this seriously?

It wasn't just eating that was out of whack; it was exercise outside of the ballet studio, too. I will never forget one day when I took the elevator instead of taking the stairs and one ballet classmate said to me, "Stairs burn more calories," with an evil, judging glare. I couldn't tell if she had a body-image problem or if she thought I was fat. In that environment, it was hard to know what was real and what was warped. And you really absorb all of that negative energy and start to look at yourself in the mirror in a different way.

ONE DAY DURING MY apprentice year—I remember it clearly because I was PMS-ing and feeling really bloated, so I didn't feel good about my body—one of the head ballet mistresses asked to speak with me in the hall. "Did you notice you've gained weight?" she asked me.

I was stunned.

Insulted.

Offended.

What an invasion of privacy. Why was an adult I wasn't close with—a boss at work—talking to me about my weight? It just felt so uncomfortable and embarrassing.

"No, I haven't noticed," I told her flatly. Because I hadn't. I was feeling a little bloated from PMS, but did that count as weight gain?

She said, "I don't know if there is anything you can cut out of your diet . . . maybe sugared soda? Do you drink that?"

"No."

"Well, cookies or whatever it is. Maybe there is just a simple thing you are eating that you can cut out. . . ." The rest of the conversation became a blur.

I had gotten a fat talk.

They happen in ballet. I had heard of them. But I never imagined I would be a victim of one.

Immediately after that talk I had to go to rehearsal for a very bouncy ballet called *Ballo*. It contains double échappés—basically a regular pointe shoe step that gets double bounced. While rehearsing this variation in front of a different ballet mistress, I danced with tears streaming down my face. I had never felt my body jiggle so much in all my life. I was so humiliated, paranoid, and depressed all at the same time. (Funny side note: This ballet mistress never confronted me about why I was upset. In her defense, maybe she was trying to spare me the humiliation of further delving into what seemed to be a horrible day. You are taught from a young age as a dancer that you leave your problems at the door and use the studio space to focus on your dancing.)

Right after the fat talk, we had a break from the company for three weeks. I went home, and with the help of my dietitian mother, I constructed a diet to get into better shape. (I felt very lucky to have my mother's expertise!) Losing weight is such a sensitive goal for a dancer, because they are already smaller than a "normal" person their age, and so they have to be very careful to lose weight healthily and not go too far. I had to cut out extra snacking and get rid of my favorite things in life: cookies and sweets. My diet now consisted of egg-white omelets, toast, and fruit for breakfast; healthy sandwiches for lunch with some healthy chips and maybe more fruit; and well-balanced dinners like the ones I grew up with (protein, starch, and a veggie). My mom told me—I later found out this is similar to Weight Watchers—that you can eat unlimited amounts of certain types of fruits and veggies. They don't count! (Well, they do, but snacking on them is very healthy and the fiber keeps your blood sugars level.) So my sugar-filled diet turned into one filled with protein, fiber, and healthy carbs. I was beginning to treat my body like an elite athlete with the ultimate goal to reach my fullest potential physically.

What wasn't so healthy was what this whole experience was doing to my mental and emotional health. While going through puberty, it is important to have some freedom to let your weight fluctuate. Hormones do insane things to your body, and the way it looks doesn't always reflect what you ate the day before. Sometimes you are just a growing hormonal human. There is nothing you have done wrong.

What ended up happening was that I kept such a close eye on my eating, because I would have done anything to be hired as an official corps member, that I overcompensated a little and ended up losing way more than I planned.

This is when I developed a strong relationship with my scale. Many people choose to stay away from the scale because it adds to their obsessiveness about their weight. But for me, it made things easier. If I knew what weight I was each morning, I didn't stare at myself obsessively in the mirror during ballet, wondering whether I was eating enough or too much. I had a clear, concrete number that didn't lie, and it took away all of the uncertainty.

Thanks to the scale, I got back to my safe goal weight, which was a little less than I'd weighed on my fat-talk day. I started to get a lot of opportunities in the company, and soon was dancing so much that I sometimes couldn't feed myself enough. During those moments, I never had to think about food. It was pure freedom, mentally, to let those worries go.

The problem was that during the off-season, or days when I had no rehearsals, I still struggled. I would find myself feeling much hungrier than usual and would spend all day long trying not to eat the world. I remember one specific day when I ate so much for lunch after company class, I stopped and counted how many calories I had had. The number was what I had aimed for in a whole day when I first was really trying to lose weight. I thought, how am I going to maintain this profession and lifestyle? It's only 1:00 p.m., and I should be done eating for the day! The magnifying glass was just too focused on my food intake and not on nourishing myself.

I went into a cycle for a year or two of overeating to the point of feeling completely disgusted with myself, and then going to the gym and restricting the next day to get back on track. The intensity of these extremes just fed off each other. I was stuck in a yo-yo scenario of always eating too much or too little. Never anything in between. It was exhausting, and I don't even know how I got through those years with the ballet success that I did. I think from the outside, I probably never looked any different. It was more of an inner mental anguish that I never could trust myself to eat properly. I started to understand that my brain was no longer in touch with my stomach, because I had tried to micromanage it so much. For a healthy eater, when they've eaten enough, their stomach kicks in and tells them they are full. But for me, that signal was completely shut off, and I never seemed to feel satisfied.

The incredible pressure and responsibility I was being given at the ballet wasn't helping. I was completely lost with my eating, and at the same time testing myself physically in rehearsals more than ever before. I remember thinking, "How come they think I can do this? I am not this good," all the time. After my debut of *Theme and Variations* with the company, I remember getting, like, four big doughnuts and eating all of them as my reward. The connection between my brain and my stomach was completely ruined. I mean, when is four doughnuts ever a good idea for anyone? These moments made me feel out of control. I knew this wasn't sustainable in terms of succeeding in my career and I had to find a way to manage the stress of my job better.

So how did I get back on track? It was a slow process. I realized that with my dance schedule, I couldn't restrict my eating so much. The restriction was what led to the bingeing. I started to give myself the things I craved before I was overly starving or desperate for a treat, and tried to practice not feeling any guilt about it. The guilt that came along with some of my eating, exacerbated by the professional expectations of what I should look like, was ruining the brain-stomach connection that I so desperately needed to find again. Little by little, by allowing myself to have more normal meals and not beating myself up for it, my obsession over what I was eating started to calm down and I started to find freedom.

I eventually settled into a much healthier relationship between my mind and my stomach. A meal is not something to feel guilty about, but something to enjoy. I now set a place mat down every time I have a meal, and always plate my food instead of eating on the run. It is a moment to be experienced and enjoyed. I make sure I have a bit of all the healthy food groups and, yes, I eat dessert. But I eat in a relaxed enough way, and slowly enough, that I can tell when I am full now and would rather stop than continue and feel stuffed. This truly took years of practice, and it involved being more gentle with myself throughout the process.

Now that I have found this mind-stomach connection, I feel completely at peace. Food doesn't stress me out like it used to. I can eat out with friends and not worry about finding the right thing on the menu or eating in front of others. If I'm hungry I eat a good-sized meal, and if I'm not I choose a salad. I feel well-adjusted and healthy.

The important lesson that every dancer needs to understand is that to be your most successful, you need to be in peak physical shape. It's about lean muscle, stamina, and strength, and you do have to eat and exercise in a certain way to get there. But there is a limit in both directions. You can eat too little and struggle to maintain muscle tone and not have enough energy to push yourself physically, whether in a performance, rehearsal, or just a class. And you can also eat too much, making it hard to be light on your feet or even get high off the ground in a jump.

For me, freedom was about not letting food control me. Every food choice I made became more of a ritual and something to be enjoyed instead of eaten quickly, in shame. When you take time to enjoy each meal without any guilt, and make good choices but also treat yourself from time to time, your relationship with food will begin to heal.

THANKFULLY NOT EVERY JOB REQUIRES one to maintain a certain fitness level, but we all have to make sacrifices and meet certain requirements for our careers. For writers, it's staying home on the weekends to write; for actors, it's going to many auditions without getting a role; for anyone in a noncreative but competitive field, it's putting in the hours without accolades. The idea that success just happens for some is a myth. To truly succeed you have to take responsibility for what's required in your chosen field. You can't play in the big leagues if you aren't going to accept the reality of what that entails.

I had moments when I wanted to avoid that reality, when I saw people who didn't have to work as hard as me to achieve their physical goals. For example, a lot of men in the company had the opposite goal of all the women. They had to be strong and muscular so they could pick us up and partner us without getting injured, while we had to be light so they could pick us up and partner us without getting injured. So a lot of them were always trying to build muscle and keep on weight, and they would freely eat anything and everything in sight. Some could even take tons of time off, eat whatever they wanted, and still come back to work with an incredible physique. I remember eating out with friends and being so jealous that the men were ordering with such freedom: hamburgers, pasta, etc. In these moments I felt trapped by the requirements of my profession, wishing I didn't have to make the efforts necessary to be my best.

What was liberating for me was properly accepting what was expected of me and taking my real responsibilities head-on. I needed to nourish myself like an athlete, and I had to learn to find balance in my eating so that I could perform at a really high level while also not getting too much in my head about the whole process. Once I finally found peace with my eating, I suddenly felt less frustrated.

> *What was liberating for me was properly accepting what was expected of me and taking my real responsibilities head-on.*

Another part of this is making sure that we don't get distracted by the successes and talents of those around us, putting ourselves down as we focus on what others have instead of our own capabilities. I definitely believe that we all have our own unique potential. We all have our strengths. And part of the key to fulfilling that potential is not comparing ourselves to others. Your fullest potential doesn't look like the fullest potential of the person next to you. It is about embracing *your* gifts and talents, and bringing them into the light, letting them grow and flourish. If we stay focused on what we don't have, we will never maximize what we do have. We also might be focusing on what others have that we don't because we are actually afraid of what we need to do. We are deflecting blame, and not taking responsibility.

> *If we stay focused on what we don't have, we will never maximize what we do have.*

This brings me back to the two different roommates I had in the dorms when I was at SAB. Both were tall, skinny blondes. I was very good friends with each, but as I was going through my own mental battle with what puberty was doing to my body, I was constantly confronted by someone who had a whole different situation than mine. One in particular could eat anything she wanted and was a string bean, with long legs and small bones; she had the body for ballet that we all wanted. I always felt like the short, stumpy roommate compared to these statuesque friends who looked like models.

What I eventually realized was that while I was envying their genetic gifts, I had my own gifts they wished they had for ballet. Being shorter made me better coordinated and able to move more quickly. I also was a very strong dancer, something that didn't come as easily for others. Focusing on my strengths made me feel less depressed about the things I didn't have. If I hadn't learned how to pump myself up and be proud of what I brought to the table, I never would have been able to focus and achieve my goals. No one has it all. If we can concentrate on what we do have instead of what we don't have, we are able to maximize our talents and find true success.

The ironic part of this story is that the day I got promoted to principal, I was the exact same weight as I had been when I was an apprentice two and a half years earlier, getting a fat talk in the hallway. I was so eager to become whatever I thought they wanted me to be that I took a conversation about my weight too far and probably lost too much weight—almost even getting injured because of it, and then struggling with how much I should be eating for the next couple of years. I strongly believe that hormones need to fluctuate at that age, and the fact that I was the same weight in the end probably means I was fine and would have started to show more lean muscle as my career progressed.

Looking back, if I could have met with a sports nutritionist and started a healthy conversation about food, I think I would have understood at an earlier age what was expected of me as a young professional and how to accomplish it. Now they have resources in my company for these exact types of things.

I am grateful to have escaped those years without losing my mind. I have friends who couldn't win the mental struggle of eating and ballet. While anorexia and bulimia are serious mental disorders that are devastating to a person's health and well-being, I also remind people that no anorexic or bulimic person is ever successful in this industry. You inevitably get injured, and you can't maintain the strength required to do what we do every day as dancers. What is essential is for you to find the balance that comes only from being gentle with yourself and from making eating a nourishing, positive moment of every day.

Striving for the fullest version of who you can be doesn't have to make you crazy! We can be working toward our best selves in a healthy, balanced way. It's about giving ourselves permission to be human. So as you take the scary steps that are aiming you toward your goals, stay gentle and real with yourself. Does working toward being a healthy and fit dancer mean I never get to treat myself? No, because then I will go too far off the deep end and eat the world! But does that mean I'm not capable of finding a happy medium? Absolutely not!!! It becomes about mental balance: working toward your best but also not feeling guilty about treating yourself every once in a while. You can still work toward an ideal while staying sane. It is important to remember that you are only human, and to make space for that.

MANAGING
STRESS

_How can we gain control
over our stress levels when
life is stressful?_

From the audience's perspective, going to the ballet is a calming experience. They find their seat. The lights dim. The conductor walks out to the podium in the orchestra pit and takes a bow, the audience claps, and the conductor turns around to face the orchestra, beginning the evening with one hand movement. After a small overture, the curtain rises, revealing the dancers in their starting positions, and the rest is history!

Little does the audience know that what has gone on behind the scenes to make all of that happen like clockwork is an incredible feat. Sometimes things go wrong right before the curtain goes up, and with an entire audience waiting, you can imagine the stress that might ensue.

One night when I was in the corps de ballet, the lead male dancer of *Tschaikovsky Piano Concerto No. 2* pulled out of the show just five minutes before the curtain was scheduled to rise. He came up to Rosemary Dunleavy, the head ballet mistress, and told her that he couldn't dance because his calf was suddenly seriously injured. Redoing an entire thirty-minute ballet without the male lead in five minutes would cause a heart attack for anyone else, but Rosemary never lost her cool. She gathered the twenty-eight other dancers performing in the ballet and quickly explained a new order that involved removing all the partnering moments the male lead was supposed to have with his partner. She also had to call the conductor from the pit to come up to the stage to notify him which parts of the score would need to be cut. This incredible undertaking, which included quick edits to every section involving the injured dancer and some ingenious fixes in which the soloist girl would fill in for the missing elements, required perfect knowledge of everyone's choreography and steps—not to mention that she had to explain all the changes to the entire cast of dancers, minutes before curtain. I have to admit that as someone in the corps that night, these last-minute changes were really thrilling and exciting, but I cannot imagine the stress involved when you are the one who is supposed to figure it all out in just a few minutes.

George Balanchine must have been aware of Rosemary's ability to stay composed under great amounts of pressure, because ten years into Rosemary's own career as a dancer at City Ballet, he asked her to be his full-time ballet mistress and assistant. Throughout her five decades as the company's main ballet mistress, Rosemary has had to deal with many similar occasions, and she is known for her impeccable response to all these moments of high stress. She never panics—she stays calm, which allows her to think of all the best possible solutions to a problem. She reacts quickly, with steely composure, without letting the stress of the moment rush her. We all feel safer under her leadership.

WITNESSING ROSEMARY SAVE THE DAY over and over always amazed me, especially as I began to struggle with my own extreme reactions to moments of high stress. As I started to take on more and more responsibility (and stress) in my career, I started to also notice a strange pattern of fainting episodes.

I've always been what you might call a lightweight. Quick to faint, tipsy after only part of a drink, moments of light-headedness when I stand up too quickly after lying down. This is due to a combination of hereditary low blood pressure (my dad always had to be careful to stand up slowly, too) and the extreme stress of my career. Having such low blood pressure makes me vulnerable to extra amounts of stress that might push me over the edge to unconsciousness.

Every time I passed out in my twenties, there seemed to be a different explanation, like my fear of needles or hospitals, so I didn't immediately label my issue as one of high stress—I just figured I had some triggers. I passed out at doctor appointments, acupuncture appointments, when dealing with the stomach flu, when cutting my finger accidentally, and when I was dropped by my partner in a rehearsal and hit my head hard on the floor.

But I wasn't just fainting—I was also having a physical panic attack every time I woke up. Every time I passed out, I would experience the sensation that I was on the edge of the universe, about to fall off into oblivion, and I would panic. I would try to come back to the real world but I felt trapped, and I would start screaming at the top of my lungs over and over again (a real joy for passersby to witness). After I was finally able to see my surroundings and realize where I was and what had happened, I often still had so much adrenaline left over from the panic attack that it would take me a while to stop screaming. Sometimes these episodes were so disorienting that I would throw up after regaining consciousness. That panicked feeling I had while being out would haunt me for days afterward (imagine not being able to shake your most horrific nightmare), and the episodes took so much of my energy that for the next day or two, I would be as limp as a noodle, feeling like I didn't even have the energy to hold myself up properly.

One moment in particular made me realize that I had a complete lack of control over the stress in my life. In the middle of a performance season, I went to dinner with a couple of friends one Monday at a restaurant (ironically called Rosemary's) in Greenwich Village. I was super tired, but I was looking forward to relaxing and catching up with my girlfriends.

At the end of the meal, one of my friends excused herself to go to the bathroom. When she came back, she was holding her finger and told us how she had just accidentally smashed it in the bathroom door. She was in intense pain and felt faint, so we rushed to the waiter to ask for some juice to help her stay conscious. We were able to "stabilize" her, thankfully. Taking a deep breath, she said, "Oh my god, that was terrifying. I don't know how you ever deal with feeling faint, Megan."

I replied, "I know, it's the absolute worst." And then I collapsed on the floor of the restaurant. This is not fiction, folks. I actually fainted from sympathizing with someone else's pain. Never before had I fainted just from watching someone else go through a scary experience.

I woke up minutes later to the EMTs coming to help me off the floor. Our girls' night out ended with us all in an ambulance that was taking me to the hospital for some tests. I usually dismissed my fainting as the result of obvious triggers, but it was now clearly getting out of control. And because it took me a day or two to recover, it was often interrupting my work, and I had a responsibility in my job to keep it from happening again. Something had to change in my life, but I was at a loss for where to start.

EVERY TIME I WAS TAKEN to the hospital after an episode, they would first assume I was anorexic, which was the usual response to someone as thin as a ballet dancer. I would tell them everything I had eaten the day before, and they would say, "Oh, OK, I guess you're not anorexic!" Then they would give me a pregnancy test. When that came back negative, they always wanted to draw blood, which was the worst thing to do, because many times it was the idea of a needle or blood that had made me pass out in the first place. By lying down and just trying to stay calm, I would survive the blood test, but the results never offered any answers. Oftentimes the doctors would give me an IV just to get me feeling better, and then eventually they would let me leave.

I was so frustrated that I was willing to try anything and everything that could perhaps help. I tried to address every possible problem. Was it my eating? Was I getting the right nutrition, enough water, to sustain my physical job? I saw a nutritionist and we brainstormed possible fixes, like adding more salt to my diet to help keep my blood pressure at a safer level, eating a banana a day for magnesium, and always keeping an extra healthy snack with me so I never ran the risk of having low blood sugar.

While I'm sure adjusting my diet was helpful, I knew that the fix that I was looking for had to be something more life changing. The fact that my episodes seemed to creep up out of nowhere really added to my anxiety. The fear of an attack eventually became a trigger in and of itself. If I started to get nervous about something, my mind would race, especially when I was in public spaces. "You cannot pass out here," I would tell myself. "Keep it together, Megan!" I knew deep down that nutrition wasn't going to be a complete solution to this problem. I couldn't just eat a banana when something started to stress me out—it would already be too late. I needed to find a way to decrease my stress level and boost my coping abilities at all times, so that I would be more resilient and I would be able to prevent attacks from occurring.

The solution ended up coming out of left field. One day

Rosemary, the queen of composure, pulled me aside to discuss a plan she had to help me with my episodes. She had to replace me whenever these events took me out of commission at work, and she wanted to help me learn to cope better. She suggested trying Transcendental Meditation, or TM. She had been practicing it since the seventies, when it was trendy thanks to the Beatles. I had heard of it before, as my uncle practiced it, but as soon as someone I really trusted in my professional setting suggested it for my health, I started to take it more seriously. One of the reasons I trusted Rosemary was because of how well she was known for dealing with and handling stress in our work environment.

Rosemary adjusted my rehearsal schedule to give me time to attend the TM lessons, and I found a local teacher. TM is a method of meditation that is taught in a methodical way to help you learn how to let go of thoughts effortlessly. The idea is that by slowing down the mind we release stress and heal the body and mind, so that after meditating we are able to resume our activities with clarity, intention, and energy. Learning TM involves a ritual of making an offering of flowers and fruit to sanctify the occasion. It might sound funny, but it helps to make the moment special, and prepares you to take the practice seriously. After the little ceremony, my teacher gave me a mantra—everyone has a different one, and you are supposed to keep it to yourself—and after some initial advice she left me in the room alone for twenty minutes.

Normally, the idea of sitting quietly for twenty minutes would seem impossible, making me feel fidgety when I didn't even feel fidgety before. But somehow, armed with my teacher's guidance and my new mantra, I was able to last the twenty minutes without a problem, even with the distraction of a loud fire engine passing by outside. I vividly remember my drive home. I didn't turn on the radio, and I didn't call anyone through my car's speakerphone. I just drove in silence and felt content about it. When I spoke to someone for the first time after that first meditation session, I realized I was so relaxed that my voice had actually lowered in tone.

I think we often don't know we are operating in a stressed-out space until we are able to come out of it. It was a huge eye-opener to me that I had different levels I could function on, and that through meditation, I could drop down into a calmer state. Was this the solution to my fainting problem? Maybe. But the only way to know for sure was to experience something that might have normally triggered me to pass out, and to see if I could stay calm and make it through to the other side.

So I meditated twice a day, and I waited. Even if I wasn't yet sure whether the TM was preventing me from passing out, it was already proving to have other benefits. My partner at the time told me he noticed a drastic difference in my regular state. The way I approached life was slower and calmer. I didn't even realize I was acting differently.

I LEARNED TM TO HELP with my stress and fainting episodes, but what I didn't know was also how much it would help me be open to opportunities that would help me grow as a person. Before TM I didn't say yes to anything out of my comfort zone. Suddenly I had a new perspective on life that made me willing to try new things. Shortly after I'd begun practicing TM, I received a very out-of-the-blue email about a show that would be opening on Broadway soon. It was a revival of the musical *On the Town*, about three sailors who are on shore leave for twenty-four hours and are looking for some girls to spend the time with. They were still looking to cast the role of Miss Turnstiles and wanted to know if I was interested in auditioning. I was very honored to receive such an email, but also aware of my limitations, so I told them, "Thanks but no thanks. I'm not a singer."

"Oh, it doesn't call for principal singing," the casting director responded. "You are in a singing lesson for part of the show." In other words, it didn't matter if I wasn't great at singing, because that was part of the role. But I still thought to myself, "This is not what I do. I'm a ballerina." I had never dreamed of going to Broadway. It just wasn't on my radar, and I felt embarrassed to even entertain the idea.

The next morning, I woke up and after meditating realized I had nothing to lose. I was at a point in my career where I was craving a new challenge. I was the go-to dancer for anything technical and Balanchine, but when it came to more creative works, I was never on the shortlist. I was always hoping to be involved in new choreography, and constantly disappointed when the rehearsal schedule came out and I was never one of the dancers picked. I suddenly realized that this Broadway opportunity was my chance to try something new, even if it did not come in the package I expected. If I couldn't say yes to a Broadway audition, how could I complain about not getting to work with new choreographers when they came to work for my company? So I changed my mind and replied to the casting director, "Sure, I'll audition!"

Next thing I knew, I was in a whirlwind of learning my audition material and finding a fifties-era outfit that would be appropriate for Miss Turnstiles. I sang the audition song around the house for the next forty-eight hours, figuring if I couldn't sing in front of my significant other, I would never be able to do it in front of strangers. It was pretty bad at first. Sometimes I wonder if this was the beginning of the end of my first marriage!

As I entered Pearl Studios on Eighth Avenue and Thirty-Sixth Street in Manhattan on the day of the audition, I saw a group of people leaving a different audition. They were all dressed alike, and I suddenly felt like I was in an episode of *Smash*, that TV show about auditioning for Broadway. It was an out-of-body experience. What the hell was I doing? I was a principal dancer with NYCB, and I had taken my day off to dress up in a Halloween costume and go put myself in a totally vulnerable space. I had become a master of my art form, and here I was attempting something that I wasn't skilled at. I was one big ball of nerves.

Other people had already done second callbacks for their roles in the show, so I was a last-minute idea—one of the last people they were seeing—and because of this, everyone important to the show was there at my audition. The lead was even there to play his role in my scene. I remember thinking, "Oh, great. So it's not just the director, choreographer, casting director, and producer who are here to watch me—I have to make a fool of myself in front of a legit actor!"

We did the acting scene first, and after my first line, the director laughed out loud! He seemed to be into my portrayal of the character, or maybe it was just the tone of my voice that made him laugh. Either way, it encouraged me to press forward confidently, as this was in fact a musical comedy and I felt that I was on the right track. After the scene they asked me to sing, and I struggled to hide how nervous I was. I had planned to put my arms up at one point in the song, but when the moment arrived, I couldn't lift them without showing how shaky my hands were, so I held them together in front of my body so no one could see my nerves. I finished the song, and it was good enough. I was just glad that part was over and that my voice hadn't cracked or anything horribly embarrassing like that.

Then they said, "OK! Let's see you dance!" I had been so focused on my acting and singing that I'd forgotten that they might want to see my dancing. I had assumed my title as a principal dancer with NYCB was enough. So there I was, suddenly learning the choreography for Miss Turnstiles, without having warmed up my body all day long! If I hadn't been so capable as a dancer, this would have been disastrous, but I was able to pull off what I needed to. We finished the dance with a coupé jeté manège and fouetté turns, basically nightmare choreography if you haven't properly warmed up. I nailed it, but not without sweating buckets, because I hadn't been properly warm to start. My cute fifties hair and makeup were starting to make me look like a drowned rat.

Just a couple of minutes later, they said to me with a smile, "We'd like to offer you the role!" I had gone to the audition with the sole goal of getting myself out of my comfort zone. I had never thought about the possibility that I might get the part! The director said to me, "This will be your Broadway debut! How exciting!" Little did he know inside I was still processing that I had even shown up to the audition.

Thankfully, my boss at NYCB was supportive of me and could tell I was excited to try something new. I went on a leave of absence from the ballet for what I thought might be a month or two, as no one knows the longevity of a Broadway show. It turned into an entire year. Throughout the rehearsal process, I continued to use my TM and embrace a "What do you have to lose?" mindset as I tried to sing and act for the first time in my life. Before trying TM, I definitely would have been too humiliated to even entertain the possibility of embarrassing myself in front of my castmates. But instead I was able to find the whole experience liberating. I found that when I wasn't chronically operating at my highest stress level, there was more room for me to be open to new possibilities.

I found that when I wasn't chronically operating at my highest stress level, there was more room for me to be open to new possibilities.

In the middle of that Broadway year, my coping skills were put to the test when one of my dogs accidentally bit my finger really hard. As my finger started to swell and bleed, I went into full-on panic mode, feeling all the symptoms of one of my episodes coming back to haunt me. My hearing started to feel distant, and I got light-headed and really hot. By this point I had learned that if I felt faint, I should get on the ground so that if I did pass out, I wouldn't hit my head, and also that keeping my body temperature cool was key. So I crawled on the floor to my bathroom and turned on a cold shower. Sitting there in my clothes, lying down on the bottom of the shower floor, I realized that I was overcoming a moment of true panic for the first time. I had done it. I had conquered what would have before been a trigger.

FOR ME, TM is what helps ground me and keeps me from feeling too stressed. But for others, stress relief might come in a different form. My good friend Sara Mearns, another principal dancer in

NYCB, just needs some quiet time alone, preferably outside. She also loves a good cry to release all of her tension. Another friend prefers to take some time to cook or clean. But no matter what form it takes, you need to be able to take some quiet time where you have space from the noise of life. A time when your mind can calm down, stop thinking, and gain some perspective. Getting mental space from the problem or task in front of you is key.

> *No matter what form it takes, you need to be able to take some quiet time where you have space from the noise of life. A time when your mind can calm down, stop thinking, and gain some perspective. Getting mental space from the problem or task in front of you is key.*

I visualize stress as a lot like being forced to hike near the edge of a cliff. When we are in the thick of it, we feel we have no options: there is a huge wall on our left side, and then just one foot to the right, the cliff drops off into a huge freefall. It feels like we are so close to teetering off the edge. What we need is something to take us back. Something to open the trail up and remove the wall that is forcing us closer and closer to the edge.

When I meditate, I feel like that wall disappears and is replaced by a huge beautiful field between me and the edge of the cliff. I have space on all sides of me, I can breathe easy, and I feel safe. The danger didn't go away, as I can still see the edge of the cliff in the distance, but it's not so close that I don't know how to deal with it. In other words, what meditation does for me is give me enough mental space to bring me back from that cliff's edge. With this newfound perspective, I can see how limited my thinking was when I was at the cliff's edge and struggling. We all need a tool that can make us suddenly feel safe and at peace. It's not important what that tool is, but it is important that you find one that works for you, sooner rather than later! If you are struggling to find one, I suggest trying some form of meditation.

It's also important to remember that feeling stress and panic is normal. The goal isn't necessarily to never feel these things. It's to gain coping mechanisms so that we don't allow them to rule our lives or define us. Stress isn't really the problem—it's that in the moment we are often too close to the problem to know how to fix it.

We all have limits to the amount of stress we can deal with. Each one of us, if pushed too much to our limits, has a different way in which our body kicks in to cope and "save" us. For me, my body was trying to cope with stress by fainting. The reason I had originally chosen to learn TM was so that I could learn how to bring my stress level down a couple of notches. That way, I wouldn't always be so close to my limit, and when a trigger occurred, I would still have room for my stress level to rise within a safe range. I knew I wouldn't be able to completely avoid or control triggers in my life, but I could make sure that when they occurred, I wasn't already operating at such a high level of stress that the trigger would push me past my limits.

> *I knew I wouldn't be able to completely avoid or control triggers in my life, but I could make sure that when they occurred, I wasn't already operating at such a high level of stress that the trigger would push me past my limits.*

It turned out that not only did TM dramatically decrease my stress levels, it also had another benefit: it opened me up to saying yes to opportunities I normally would have rejected. Because of TM, I said yes to an opportunity to go on Broadway, which turned into a year that would alter the entire course of the rest of my life. And without TM, I would not have been open to other changes that would improve my life in ways I could never have imagined. Meditation opened me up to a way of existing that I didn't know was possible—one in which I could manage my emotions and conquer my most extreme fears.

HANDLING
FEEDBACK

⌭

*How can we keep ourselves
from getting upset about
negative feedback?*

I remember the first time I read a review of my dancing. I had just joined NYCB as an apprentice and danced Snow and Spanish in my first couple of performances of *The Nutcracker*. Some friends of mine showed me a ballet forum where someone had mentioned my name in a positive way, saying they were looking forward to seeing me dance more. To my friends, I just chuckled, pretending it was no big deal, but on the inside, I was basking in the glory. Someone out there who didn't even know me had plucked me out of the corps de ballet and admired my dancing! Their comment gave me a real boost of confidence, and I let my sense of accomplishment power me through the rest of my *Nutcracker* shows.

What I didn't realize, but would soon painfully learn, was that if you give weight to positive reviews, you will have to give equal importance and weight to the negative ones. And there will be negative ones. Two years later, I was promoted to soloist, incredibly young—only nineteen years old—and this same forum had a couple of posts about how I did not deserve my promotion. They thought there were other dancers who deserved the next round of promotions more than I did. I agreed with them that my promotion was early, but I had already proven myself dancing the lead in a full-length ballet that summer when all the other principals were injured. Reading these comments, I suddenly became aware of how some people were rooting for certain dancers at the expense of others. It made me feel like I had been pitted against my colleagues. I felt defensive of my promotion, and under pressure to prove myself to these strangers on the Internet.

> *What I didn't realize, but would soon painfully learn, was that if you give weight to positive reviews, you will have to give equal importance and weight to the negative ones. And there will be negative ones.*

Just one year later, I was promoted again. I was a principal at age twenty. Now, the people coming to see me perform would be expecting principal-quality work. Being promoted prematurely is hard for a dancer. When you are a corps member and you get a special part, the audience sees you as the underdog and roots for you. But when you are promoted quickly, the audience's expectations are much higher, and they think to themselves, "Well, let's see if she's actually got it. . . ." I was a principal at the same time as legendary ballerinas Darci Kistler and Kyra Nichols were finishing out their careers. The idea that I was supposed to perform at their level was incredibly unrealistic and stressful to me. I had only joined the company three years before!

Soon after I was promoted, my partner Joaquín and I were told that we would be dancing the lead roles in Balanchine's *Theme and Variations* the next month. For those not well versed in Balanchine ballets, the female role in *Theme and Variations* is an incredible feat of technical mastery at the highest of speeds. There is no room for error. The first variation for the female lead is danced only up and down the center line of the stage. If you misplace your weight just once, your steps will move off the line, and you'll risk running into the corps de ballet on either side of you while also ruining the symmetrical view that the audience is supposed to see. And once that first variation starts, there is no moment to catch your breath or find your balance again. Each step leads directly into the next, a hallmark of Balanchine technique. In other types of classical choreography, you might have a step or two to connect all the larger movements, but in Balanchine technique, we are trained to edit out all those extra steps and connect one large movement directly to the next. This means that your landing from one step becomes the preparation for the next one. If you land wrong, you'll start the next step wrong, too, so being a little off on just one step could prove disastrous by the end of the variation.

The second variation, which is just as fast and technically difficult, finishes with a complex series of turns in the front panel of the stage. This is notoriously the hardest place to turn—you are keenly aware of the orchestra pit just below you, and the lights are much brighter and more distracting in the front of the stage. So your impulse is to lean back and away from both of these obstacles. What's more, the final moment of the variation is the beginning of the pas de deux. If your second variation has finished well, your pas de deux will seem to just coast. But if it hasn't finished well, you are spending the whole long and difficult pas de deux trying to overcome the disappointment over what just happened in your variation.

They were the most difficult steps ever thrown my way. But in addition to learning and mastering them, I also had to pull a commanding ballerina stage presence, worthy of this legendary ballet with its gorgeous classical tutu and tiara and the chandeliers above us, out of nowhere. It was the ultimate, most complicated diva role in our repertoire, and I was nobody's twenty-year-old diva. I was naive, still very much showing my Utah upbringing. I didn't yet have a stage presence that screamed "Look at me *or else*," that magnetic pull that an experienced artist commands from the audience the minute they step on stage.

For most of my short career up until then, whenever I was cast in something new and possibly stressful, I always said to myself,

"Well, at least it's not *Theme and Variations*!" That tactic doesn't work when the big, scary thing actually IS *Theme and Variations*. How could I reason myself out of the stress on this one?!

The rehearsal process was very defeating for me. I cried in my dressing room after every rehearsal for the two weeks leading up to the first show. Sobbed. I was struggling with the physical pain that comes from pushing your body to its limits. At that time in my career, I hadn't yet discovered all of the proper body maintenance that allows one to push through difficulties day after day. I kept straining my inner thigh muscles, and I was stuck in a cycle of overeating and then undereating that didn't make rehearsals any easier. I wasn't confident in my body, and I felt out of shape in many of the rehearsals.

I didn't get why this role, which felt completely beyond my years of experience, had been given to me. I couldn't believe my bosses thought I could do it. Meanwhile, Joaquín was thrilled. Eight years my senior, he was ready for this moment and soaking up every minute of it. His enthusiasm made me feel even worse. I remember sitting on the ground fixing my pointe shoes after class on the day of our first performance in DC. He was so excited, and he came over to me and asked, "How you doing?!" I thought about just letting it out—crying and showing him how nervous I was. But instead I just smiled and answered with a very nonbelievable, "Great!" I felt incredibly alone in my nerves, my fear, and my stress.

In the end, the shows went well. I might have double-hopped

a landing of a pirouette here and there, but in all honesty, the actual first performance is an incredible blur. My mom had suggested to me that maybe if I didn't feel confident enough to be my own diva ballerina, I should mimic another one in the company. Miranda Weese was the brilliant ballerina I had to look up to, and I did many shows just pretending I was Miranda, not Megan, commanding the stage.

After that tour I was spent, so I treated myself with one of my new principal paychecks to a yoga retreat in upstate New York. For a week, I was surrounded by women fifteen to twenty years older than me who were there for a whole gamut of reasons—from midlife crises to recovering from a divorce to just wanting a relaxed week away with a friend. I will never forget meeting two middle-aged gals who befriended me. They were the bad girls of the retreat, sneaking in wine and a TV to their cabins. When they asked me why I was there, I realized how funny it was to answer, "I got promoted," as though it was a horrible thing. I always had to follow up with a description of how my promotion was adding to the stress in my life, and how I felt overwhelmed by the responsibilities expected of me. But being around people who were going through more serious life moments really put my troubles into perspective. I started to look at the bright side of my situation and gave myself a much-needed pat on the back.

I returned to New York City feeling refreshed and ready to tackle my new, difficult job again. Over the next couple of years, I was repeatedly tested with this same ballet. Each time I gained a little more confidence as my technique started to become more and more consistent. Once the technical side felt easy, then I could start to loosen up my artistry and really embrace the ballerina in me.

I remember one performance in particular at the end of a winter season. I was so proud with how I performed, and I truly felt that everything I was capable of was left out there on that stage. I was so confident I actually thought, "I bet the reviewers noticed." The next morning, I went looking for a review of my show in the *New York Times*.

The *Times* had recently hired a new head ballet critic, Alastair Macaulay. He had an incredible amount of knowledge about the history of the art form. Reading his reviews, I always learned something new about a ballet's background. But he also loved to be ruthless in his judgment and criticism of dancers. He obviously loved some of us, and greatly disliked others. It seemed certain dancers could do no wrong, and the rest of us would just never measure up no matter how hard we tried. I was in the second category. I wasn't alone: he was harsh toward most of us at that time.

Looking for that review was a big mistake. It was a recap of the whole season, and while Alastair didn't say anything completely horrendous about me, he didn't say anything nice, either. His criticism of me at that time was that I was too saccharine, like cotton candy. (If you want to improve your vocabulary, just read a ballet review! I will admit that sometimes I didn't know if my reviews were good or bad when I read them—I had to look up the meaning of the words that had been used to describe me.) I was in a diva role, and "cotton candy" was not going to cut it.

It was a Monday morning, the first day off after a long, hard season, and I felt like all the energy and work I had put into my job the last couple of months was a complete waste. It was just one too many bad reviews of my dancing. Sometimes, if you know you didn't dance your best, reading a bad review isn't all that shocking. But when you feel like you couldn't have done any better, and you are so proud of yourself for how far you have come, and you read a bad review . . . well, let's just say you start to question how much longer you can maintain a positive attitude in this line of work. I even started thinking I didn't want to dance anymore. What was it all worth anyway if I was going to punish myself day in and day out, and then not be appreciated in the end?

As scary as live performances are, there is something that feels safe about the fact that no one can rewind what they just saw and show it to someone else. It's a small moment in time, and if it doesn't go well, no one can watch it in order to criticize it over and over again. But thanks to the Internet, reviews do last forever now. They follow you. I kept wondering why my time as a principal had to coincide with this crochety old British man who was obviously not a fan of mine. Previous dance reviewers for the *Times* were less negative in their critiques, adopting the philosophy "If you don't have something nice to say, don't say anything at all." But Alastair's reviews were nasty and painful, and I was miserable. I couldn't do any better than I'd done in that last show, and it still wasn't good enough for this man who was going to write an immortal review of my performance for everyone to read. I kept thinking that people I knew in Utah who might have been wondering how my career was going would search for reviews of my dancing and find these. It was humiliating to be critiqued negatively in such a national way.

I decided enough was enough, and I needed to stop obsessing over my reviews. But first I wanted to make sure that they weren't a sign that I needed to do something differently. So I scheduled a meeting with my boss, Peter Martins. At that time, he had been head of the company for almost twenty-five years, and he had seen countless ballerinas tackle the roles I was trying to accomplish. He was also the one pushing me faster than I felt I should be pushed. He obviously had faith in my ability and potential, and his support was the main thing that kept me going in my moments of doubt. "Well, if he thinks I can do it, there must be something there," was a constant thought running through my head during these times.

"I don't know if you are aware, but I get horrible reviews," I told him in our meeting. "Not one of them has been good recently and I'm getting to a point where I can't take it anymore. It's made me not want to dance, and as that's not what I truly want, I've decided to completely stop reading them and look the other way.

It's the only way I can continue doing what I love. But before I put on the blinders, and just focus on myself, I want to make sure you don't see any truth to these reviews. Is there something I'm missing? Is there something I need to develop or work more on?"

I was truly ready to take real feedback from my boss and implement whatever it was he suggested. You can't ask this type of question and not be open to hearing the bad with the good. I trusted him, and I was ready to take whatever he told me and work on it to the nth degree.

I will never forget his shocking response: "Don't change a thing!" He went on to tell me he gets bad reviews for his new ballets all the time, and if he focused on that, he would be miserable, too. He told me, "What matters is the people in our circle. Your ballet masters, your partners, your director. We know the work you are putting into yourself. We are here for the process. This guy on the outside, he has no idea what you are dealing with and how you are working to grow. If you focus on him, you will never be happy."

And with that, a huge sense of relief washed over me. He was right. How could I give this one person all the power to decide whether I was measuring up? He was only one opinion out of 2,500 other people in the audience for that show. Sure, he was the head dance critic for the *New York Times*, but wasn't I dancing for every person out there in the audience? My dancing had started to become this effort to please this one man I had never met. Seeking his validation had become an obsession, and it was time to move on.

And so I put the blinders on. I literally kept the visual in my head of a horse with its blinders attached to its harness. I needed to really imagine looking straight in front of me, and not letting myself indulge in seeking out validation on the Internet. I wasn't going to get where I needed to go if I wasted any more time being distracted by things in my peripheral vision. My therapist liked to say, "Keep your eyes on your own yoga mat," and I used that visual to help me focus as well.

> *I wasn't going to get where I needed to go if I wasted any more time being distracted by things in my peripheral vision.*

It's worth mentioning here that there's a big difference between feedback from a boss and feedback from an outsider. I could learn to ignore the opinions of reviewers, but Peter's feedback was important for me to hear. And when a boss or teacher gives us feedback, it's not always good news. In these situations, we have to listen and keep an open mind but not let the criticism take us down. We have to ask ourselves, "While this might have been hard to hear, was it constructive criticism, aimed at helping me achieve my greatest potential? Or was it just criticism about something I do not have control over and should not be changing?" We have to know our own worth and remember the work that we have put in. When it is constructive criticism, hearing things you don't want to hear from an authority figure can actually be a good exercise. If that person is a good boss, they are giving you information that you can implement to change your work for the better. It should be inspiring, because it means they see potential in you!

> *Hearing things you don't want to hear from an authority figure can actually be a good exercise . . . because it means they see potential in you!*

It is important to speak up and ask for specifics if you feel totally lost about implementing their feedback. What are actionable steps you can take to make this happen? Do they have any advice on how you can perform those steps? And if they don't, you should find someone else who does, such as a colleague you admire. No one does everything right all of the time. A really defensive person who isn't open to course-correcting won't ever fulfill their potential.

Sometimes, our superiors are not sure exactly what needs to be changed, and so they might suggest the wrong thing. When this happens, it's helpful to take their advice with a grain of salt, and take a step back to analyze the problem for yourself. We need to be able to know ourselves best, and at the same time be open to making change happen when it is suggested by someone whose opinion we value. For years, certain ballet masters would shout out the same corrections to me over and over again. I would implement what they were saying, but they were still never happy. It wasn't until another person corrected the same thing in a different way that I was able to understand what needed to be fixed. The boss isn't always right in their advice of *what* needs to be changed, but we should stay open to the fact that *some* kind of change needs to occur.

> We need to be able to know ourselves best, and at the same time be open to making change happen when it is suggested by someone whose opinion we value.

IT'S HARDER THAN YOU might think to avoid a review about yourself in the *New York Times*. Sometimes friends would even call or text me to tell me that they were so sorry about the bad review I received. Those were frustrating moments, because while those people were doing their best to support me through what they thought might be a rough time, they were actually telling me news I didn't really want to know. It would have been much better to be kept in the dark! I had to train all of the people in my life to avoid reviews just as I was doing, or at least to not tell me about them. I even received fan mail coming to my defense. There was one woman in particular, from Queens. She meant well, and I actually saved her letters because it felt good to have that support. But I never let her letters, or the texts and calls from friends, push me to actually read a review. As soon as I realized they were about to tell me about a review, good or bad, I would skim the rest of the letter, almost reading it with my hands covering my eyes.

At first, it was scary to avoid reading reviews, as I still kind of cared what Alastair Macauley and others thought about my dancing. Without knowing what was being written about me, I assumed the worst . . . obviously! That's what any perfectionist would do! But eventually I got really good at not caring. My commitment to ignoring the noise became even stronger when I realized that as a person in the entertainment industry myself, I should understand that these reviewers and critics were engaging in their own form of entertainment. Their biggest responsibility was to sell papers, and I had *zero* business engaging in their efforts to do so. I came to realize how far apart our goals and missions were. And by separating their jobs as critics from my job as a dancer, I came to respect their work.

> I realized that as a person in the entertainment industry myself, I should understand that these reviewers and critics were engaging in their own form of entertainment. Their biggest responsibility was to sell papers.

As time went on, and I matured in my roles, I started to get better reviews—or so I was told. It makes me laugh because I was so disciplined in my efforts to not buy into the reviews anymore that at first, when people would tell me I got a positive review, I would almost react the same as if it was a negative one. I would shudder and immediately try to stop listening to what they were saying to me, even though it was actually good news. But I learned to graciously say, "Thank you, but I don't read them. If you buy into the good ones, then you have to buy into the bad ones!"

It was liberating to be free of the constant validation-seeking that had possessed my dancing in those beginning years. To step on stage and not be thinking of that one person who was going to write about me was a wonderful thing. I was able to truly dance for myself and enjoy each moment without thinking constantly about the adjective I had been limited to in the previous day's paper. I'm sure this made my dancing better. The old me would be tempted to go back and look for validation online, but I knew that it was a vicious cycle, and I never wanted to go back there again.

I think a big part of my frustration with my early reviews was that for every bad review I got, someone else in my company got a glowing one. And the real shame was that I was jealous of their success. Why couldn't I be glorified like that? I was putting in just as much work! But when you give power to those voices, you take power away from yourself: your power to achieve your fullest potential. You need to focus instead on working on your own personal strengths and setting your own personal goals. And only you will know when you've achieved those goals. You shouldn't rely on someone else to tell you when you've made it to the finish line.

You need to focus . . . on working on your own personal strengths and setting your own personal goals. And only you will know when you've achieved those goals. You shouldn't rely on someone else to tell you when you've made it to the finish line.

When I look at my students, I realize how different every dancer is. Each one is blossoming at their own rate. No one *should* be on anyone else's time line, and as long as they're putting in the proper effort and their motivation is coming from the right place, improvement will come. You can't make it happen just because it's happening to the person next to you. It will happen when you have individually dug deep and done the work. And then have some patience as you allow it to develop on its own, without judging when it should arrive. You must work on the basics and your foundational strength before you can expect any true growth to happen. A dancer's leg doesn't just suddenly get higher because their friend's did. It gets higher because they strengthen and stretch it more.

This brings me to one of my most important realizations. As I have worked hard to succeed in a very competitive and challenging industry, I have come to see potential as independent from the success of those around you. If someone next to you achieves their goals, it doesn't take away your own opportunity to achieve success. I like to imagine that we each have our own swimming lane. Someone moving ahead in the lane next to me doesn't compromise my potential to move ahead in my own lane.

I know this sounds cheesy, but a line at the end of the musical *Hamilton* has always really resonated with me. When I first heard Burr, Hamilton's biggest rival, sing at the end, "The world was wide enough for both Hamilton and me," I thought of my own industry and the way we are all working to achieve success. A critic or a colleague who you are in competition with is not going to be what keeps you from reaching your fullest potential. But focusing on them is what might. The power lies within you to achieve your greatness. All it requires is that you focus on the right things. What am *I* capable of? What are *my* talents? What do *I* want to grow that could be great in *me*?

> I have come to see potential as independent from the success of those around you. If someone next to you achieves their goals, it doesn't take away your own opportunity to achieve success.

We are all reviewed sometimes—even if the negative critic is just inside our own head, as we compare ourselves to others. But we need to focus on achieving the goals we set for ourselves—writing X number of words per day, running X number of miles, booking a new client—instead of what other people are doing or what's being said about us. If you put all of your work and energy into your own goals and fulfilling your greatest potential, you will find more satisfaction in the end, and no doubt actually achieve much more success than if you allowed yourself to get bogged down with the noise.

MODERATING
PERFECTIONISM

*How can we make our
perfectionism work for us
instead of against us?*

As far back as I can remember, I have been a perfectionist. My mom tells me that whenever I was coloring as a kid and I accidentally colored outside the lines, I would get so upset that I'd rip the page out of my coloring book, crumple it up, and throw it across the room. The jack-in-the-box was a particularly frustrating toy for me because I could never get the man stuffed back inside his box properly. I'd throw that across the room, too. (Maybe another topic we should be discussing in this book is patience, but I will admit that I have no expertise on the subject!)

I have a very vivid memory of trying to read *Little House on the Prairie* on a family camping trip. My inner narrator had to execute the lines perfectly. If I messed up the words as I said them in my head, I had to start the whole book over! A half hour passed and I was still on the first page. I remember thinking to myself, how does anyone ever read a whole book? The idea of not expecting perfection from oneself didn't even seem like an option. I didn't care if others made mistakes, but for me, as I attempted anything, the entire goal was to find perfection. It wasn't for praise, it was truly for my own satisfaction.

Being a perfectionist translates very well to the ballet world. You have to pay incredible attention to detail to become successful in this art form. There is no room for debate on what a proper fifth position is in ballet. If any of the toes from your back foot are peeking out from behind the heel of your front foot, it doesn't count as fifth position. Your feet aren't crossed enough. Every position requires that you place every part of your body in a specific way.

This is exactly what first drew me to this style of dance when I was younger. I liked that there was a wrong and a right to it. And I enjoyed the work and discipline required to be right.

From the ages of five to twelve, I attended a dance studio that focused on tap, jazz, and ballet. All of the other people in my dance class were more interested in jazz. It was the fun class. Ballet was too disciplined and lacking in freedom for most kids. I remember one day, our teacher gave us the option to skip our regular ballet barre and move straight to the more fun steps. We took a vote, and I answered honestly that I still wanted to do the barre. I was the only one. I soon realized I was the only person who loved the discipline of ballet. Every other eight-year-old found it to be like dance prison. It was the first time I started to realize that I liked ballet more than my classmates did. It was becoming my favorite way to dance. The thing that I liked to do.

I tried other things as a kid, like gymnastics and violin, and I worked just as hard at them as I did in the ballet studio. But I was so bad at the other things, and it pushed me away from them. The perfectionist in me wasn't interested in doing anything I couldn't do well. I think part of being a perfectionist is the joy you experience when you can accomplish something difficult. So I decided to commit to focusing on ballet. I wasn't yet sure what I was working toward, but I knew I liked ballet and was talented at it.

At twelve, I transitioned from my tap, jazz, and ballet studio to a full-time ballet school, the Ballet West conservatory. There, everyone else was as serious about ballet as I was. We took two ballet classes a night after school. It was a dream to be in a space where everyone was working on ballet as hard as I was. My friends and I never stopped working. When we were split up into groups during class, we didn't just stand at the back waiting for our turn—we always spent the down time working on some part of the combination by ourselves. I carpooled to class with a friend who was even more hardworking than me. She always wanted to stay half an hour late after every class to work on her jumps or turns. I was surrounded by like-minded people. It was heaven.

This dedication and focus carried me to more competitive levels in the ballet world. Auditioning for summer intensive programs all around the country, a huge part of any young dancer's training, was the next big step. I almost missed my SAB audition because I was sick at home with a cold and hadn't even gone to school that day. But I mustered up the strength, and snuck a cough drop in my mouth in between every combination at the barre so that I wouldn't cough while trying to dance. It was a good decision, because I was accepted to the program and decided to attend, and if I hadn't, my whole life might have gone differently.

I approached my first summer course at SAB with gusto. On my third day, we took class with the oldest teacher at the school, Antonina Tumkovsky. Born in 1905, she had been a soloist with the Kiev Ballet before World War II, and her Soviet style of teaching demanded the utmost in energy and stamina. Her classes were brutal, pushing dancers to their limits, and I think the only way to really get through them is to pace yourself—something I did not do in those first couple of classes. Like any proper perfectionist, I put every ounce of effort in my being into every single combination, and when class finished, I felt like I was going to throw up. I remember going down to the cafeteria and not wanting lunch for the first time in my life. My body was buzzing with exhaustion for hours after. It took me a couple of classes to realize that working at my normal level all the way through Tumy's classes would not be sustainable. I had to learn to take it with a grain of perfectionist salt.

That was a first important lesson in limits. Achieving perfection isn't possible 100 percent of the time, and we have to pick and choose when to put that effort into play. It's not always a positive thing to push ourselves past what we are capable of handling. Completely losing my appetite and taking a couple of days to recover from her class was probably not the goal my teacher had in mind. I was starting to learn how to moderate my perfectionist efforts in order to make it to the finish line.

> *Achieving perfection isn't possible 100 percent of the time, and we have to pick and choose when to put that effort into play. It's not always a positive thing to push ourselves past what we are capable of handling.*

YEARS LATER WHEN I BEGAN dancing principal roles at NYCB, one of the things I struggled with was that I was obsessed with the challenge of perfecting my technique and spent little energy on developing my stage presence. I liked ballet because of the difficult work it took to make each step correct. I wasn't in it for the drama of swan arms, or to just feel the breeze on my body as I moved through space, though I would learn to enjoy those things over time as well. But in order to be able to dance principal roles well, I needed a ballet master who could help me enjoy the artistic side of dancing.

The first person I was assigned to work with was Merrill Ashley, the ultimate perfectionist in the ballet world. Merrill was one

of the last Balanchine ballerinas (a phrase we use to refer to a ballerina who was coached and choreographed on by Mr. B. himself)
and was the ultimate Balanchine technician. Balanchine choreographed *Ballo della Regina* on her to highlight her technical clarity
and precise footwork. Merrill never had a foot or arm out of place.
Her turnout was so amazing that her legs sometimes looked like
they were attached to her body differently than everyone else's.
And she held herself to extreme standards. She pushed herself to
be the best technician there was, and had a reputation for expecting nothing less.

As amazing as it was to be in the studio with such a legend,
working with a ballet master who had an even more critical eye on
technique than I did was really hard for me. I would be expecting
perfection from myself, and then hear from her at the front of the
room that that effort needed to be doubled. Our perfectionist tendencies compounded on each other to the point where I was left
feeling scared to even move at all, for fear of stepping out of place,
or using my arms wrong. Merrill expected just as much from the
dancers she was coaching as she had expected from herself in her
own career, which was a lot!

The corrections I received over and over from Merrill were always about my upper body. My shoulders were a bit tight and
rolled forward for ballet, and my pointy elbows always seemed to
ruin the illusion that my arms were creating one round, soft line.
For months, I remember her just shouting out, "Elbows!" or "Shoulders!" I wanted to make these corrections so badly but didn't know

what to do to implement them properly into my own body. Once I did a whole performance of *Ballo* while desperately squeezing my shoulders down to make sure they didn't "pop up" and get in the way, so I could please her. I later watched the recorded video of that show and realized that whatever she was trying to get me to do, squeezing my shoulders down wasn't the solution. I looked stiff and uncomfortable and I'm sure the audience felt the same watching me.

My goal became avoiding more corrections from Merrill. How could I dance so she would ease up on me? All I wanted to do was please her. But just dancing to avoid her corrections was not going to produce my best dancing. I was becoming distracted by my effort to be perfect for her.

I will never forget the time she finally came back with some praise after a show.

"Everything we worked on looks great! You did it!" I couldn't believe I was getting a rave report from this taskmaster! I felt so validated and relieved until she said, "But . . ." I remember thinking, "Really??? We can't just leave it there for the night and celebrate that accomplishment for a moment?" I was dying to have one night where the work I had done had been enough. I was trying so hard, and the perfectionist in me needed to hear some praise.

The "but" was about my bow, a part of the performance I normally thought of as off-limits to corrections and feedback from coaches. She was finally happy with my dancing. However, as the ultimate perfectionist herself, she now wanted me to perfect my bow at the end of the performance. It was something about how she was seeing too much of the top of my head when I took my curtsy.

That was the moment in my career when I realized that as a ballet dancer, you are *never* done working. That is what we do. No matter how well a performance went one night, the next day, we are back in the studio working on it. There is always improvement to be made before the next show. But it's hard for a dancer to feel confident while performing yet be open to deconstructing their performance the next day in the studio, breaking it down in order to keep improving. Those are two conflicting mentalities: confidence in front of a large audience, and, in order to grow, humility the next day in the studio. But having the ability to express both is necessary to be a great dancer.

At the beginning of my career I found that balance to be difficult, especially if I had a big mishap onstage. Sometimes I would fall during the show in a big way and hear every person in the 2,500-seat house inhale with horror as I slapped my hands to the ground to catch myself or slid into the wings on my butt. Other times, a lift wouldn't happen, or I would miss a step, or have to hop on a turn because I wasn't on balance.

My perfectionist brain had a really hard time being okay with a less-than-perfect show, even though they happen to the best of us. Knowing you didn't leave your best out there on that stage is a difficult feeling to process when you have put hours of work into what is ultimately only a couple of shows. At the beginning of my career, when I was still figuring out that dancers are just human after all, this was especially hard to deal with. You rehearse for hours and hours for a ballet, not to mention the years of technical training required to get you to that point. When the show doesn't go well, it makes you feel like all that work you put in wasn't worth anything. A waste of time. A missed moment to show the world your ability.

The problem with being so focused on improving and perfecting my technique was that I obsessed more and more over the difficult steps in the ballets I was performing.

I thought I was doing what I was supposed to be doing, but what really ended up happening was that focusing on the problem steps made them even worse. Too much worry does not magically put you on your leg! I didn't have a good flow to my dancing. I wasn't enjoying the journey it took to get me there. And all of my personal satisfaction came from hitting a difficult partnering step or pirouette on my own with perfection. I wasn't dancing!

IN THE BALLET WORLD, we perform each ballet two to four times in a given season, so you want those few moments out there to really be your best. When I headed to Broadway and danced the same part 365 times, I was finally able to learn a whole lot about loosening my grip on perfection. The ability to be onstage so much with the same choreography but a different audience each time taught me to shed the ballet perfection brain and focus on being an entertainer.

My ballet brain was still very much turned on in the first few months of doing *On the Town*. I was not going to expect anything less than perfect from myself. Well, it turns out that it is just a universal truth that your performance is not always going to be at the same level. You might perform one moment in the show phenomenally but make a big mistake later in the same show. I had to accept that it would not be possible to be absolutely perfect for every single moment of every single show. We are human beings, and mistakes or bloopers are bound to happen when you roll the dice that many times. And so I started to embrace the idea of going home and being okay with an imperfect show.

> *It is just a universal truth that your performance is not always going to be at the same level.*

Meditation was also a big part of this process. On Broadway, there are two days a week when you have two shows a day, a matinee and an evening. Doing the same show every night is one thing, but the real lesson comes when you execute the same show more than once in a day. You can easily feel the difference in shows because they are so close together. What I started to realize was that if I meditated before the second show, my evening performances went much better. My body was right where I needed it to be, and I could stay in the moment with the live orchestra, and just let the dancing go. Those shows were so freeing, and it was a huge lesson for me to take back to ballet when my Broadway run was over.

As I practiced meditation more and more, I started to be able to be more present in my dancing. It was almost shocking to realize how before, I had only felt excited for performances to be over with and done well. I wasn't even excited to dance them. I always used to say to my colleagues as soon as the curtain was about to rise, "It's almost over, guys!" What a weird thing to think! The ballet hadn't even started yet. I just wanted the stress to be behind me.

What meditation brought me was the ability to get over my fear and dread of the scary steps. I realized how much time I had wasted dancing in a rush to get to the scary step, execute it well, move onto the bows, and head home, thinking I had achieved what I set out to do. I wasn't hearing the beautiful orchestra play. I was so in my head about trying to be perfect that I wasn't able to be in the present and enjoy the moment, allowing my dancing to flourish.

I think I was too scared of the grandiosity of it all—a sixty-piece orchestra below me and 2,500 educated New Yorkers who know what they are watching. Now I think that's amazing. But as a young dancer, I pasted on a smile, even though all I was feeling inside was fear as I plowed through my performances just to get to the end.

Not only did loosening my grip on my shows through meditation help me enjoy the process more, but I also danced better. My body eased up and felt the music. I was responding in real time, not like some robot dancing doll whose Play button was pushed when the curtain went up. I was no longer trying to control the outcome of my performances. Instead, I just prepared my body as well as I could, and then let it fly. Allowing that room for the performance to sometimes be less than perfect freed up the artistic side of my dancing and helped me blossom into my fullest artistic self.

FOR ALL OF US, it is important to know that there is no room to grow when you are afraid of being less than perfect. And we need to learn to power through our mistakes.

As I've matured, I've learned to use my perfectionist abilities only in key moments. I don't keep it turned on all the time. Especially now, as a mother, I have learned to embrace a little bit of chaos. For example, sometimes I'll clean my whole house, and then when my oldest daughter wakes up from her nap, she immediately takes every single toy out and the place is a mess again. I've learned to let the mess be. It wasn't easy, but it allows me and my family to just live and be carefree. There is no way to be a mom and have neurotic tendencies about things. You quickly learn to take your foot off the perfectionist gas pedal.

When it is helpful, I turn that perfectionist mode back on. Having great attention to detail is useful when organizing a trip. Doing my schoolwork for my MBA requires a strong effort toward perfection. And when I am in the dance studio (not on stage), working toward that ideal version of a ballet pushes me to be my best.

When I don't need perfectionism anymore, I have to consciously turn it off. Sometimes I have to meditate to help me let go of the need to do everything a certain way. But having that ability to turn it on and off is much more powerful than having it all the time.

> *Having that ability to turn [perfectionism] on and off*
> *is much more powerful than having it all the time.*

As I've gotten older, I've seen how much unhappiness striving toward perfection brought into my life. It has kept me from enjoying certain moments if they aren't going exactly as planned, sometimes even to an embarrassing extent. For example, many times while cooking a recipe, I have to take a deep breath when I have used the wrong amount of an ingredient or burned something. My perfectionist brain dominates me, and I just want to scream and start the entire recipe over. Learning to let go of that impulse is how I've learned to survive—and to allow perfectionism to work for me, instead of letting it dominate my thoughts and actions.

"Life is too short to sweat the small stuff." We are all told that, but a perfectionist hears this advice and just groans. To a perfectionist, the small stuff is everything! It's like telling us not to care at all. It's so hard to moderate these efforts. But if we are able to let go of those reins a bit and allow our perfectionist brains to come into play only when they are helpful and not harmful, imagine how much further we can go!

COMING TO TERMS
WITH FAILURE

⌘

*How can we approach failure in
a positive way instead of letting
it get us down?*

It can be hard for perfectionists to learn how to give themselves room to make mistakes so that they can take risks and grow. But it can be even harder for perfectionists to deal with actual failures. After years of achievement, I didn't experience my first real failure until I was in my thirties, and when it happened, it felt like the ultimate devastation.

In 2010, I had gotten married for the first time. Like everyone when they are getting married for the first time, I imagined our marriage would last forever. Since I was a bit of a public figure as a principal dancer with NYCB, the *New York Times* wanted to feature my fiancé and me in their weekly Vows section, which highlights a New York wedding of interest. I found out during that experience that if you still had a wonderful marriage after ten years, they would feature you again. I thought, "Oh, that is *so* happening. Our marriage is going to last." There wasn't a doubt in my mind that we would make it ten years. How could that be hard to achieve?

Fast-forward five years, and I was finishing the end of my fun year on Broadway. Before one of my last shows, I found out through a text message that my marriage was ending. The person with whom I had spent the last thirteen years, ever since I'd left the safety of the SAB dorms, was no longer my close partner. He had quickly become my enemy.

My entire world collapsed. Everything that I had believed about my home life crumbled and within a week I was putting my house on the market, giving up custody of my dogs, and trying to figure out what to do next.

Until then, I hadn't realized how much of my life had been one success after another. I just foolishly thought that if you worked hard on something and tried to make the right choices, everything would work out. Therefore, if life hadn't worked out in the ways you'd hoped, it was because you had done something wrong at a certain point along the way: you didn't plan ahead, you didn't try hard enough, or you didn't focus. I was really cutthroat in my view of what success entailed.

You see, most things had always gone my way. It wasn't without effort, but before my divorce I had never experienced a serious failure. In school, I had always received perfect grades. Once I started getting straight A's, I felt like I *had* to continue to earn them so I could maintain my perfect GPA. Sometimes, my efforts didn't even contribute toward the ultimate goal of learning; it was just about doing whatever I had to do to make sure that I was able to achieve an A in a class. It was almost a distracting obsession.

In ballet, meanwhile, from the very beginning I was always ahead of my age group. The class I danced with was mostly two years older than me. When I auditioned for the local Ballet West *Nutcracker*, I was always accepted, and performed for three years as Clara, the young child lead. Even after I left my dolly-dinkle school and headed toward more serious training, I was still in a class with people older than me. When auditions came to town, I was accepted to every single summer program, usually with a scholarship. Success wasn't so much a hope or goal as it was a given.

This isn't to say I didn't put the work in. I was not going to ever do anything less than my best, and the positive results would always be seen.

But with my divorce, my run as a perfectionist with results had come to an end. Because I had always come home to my parents with straight-A report cards and success in my dance career, telling them about the end of my marriage was one of the most difficult parts of it for me. I felt like I was letting them down for the first time ever.

I once thought that the details of the reasons for the divorce were so important, but now I realize they are not even worth sharing. Once you get some perspective from a situation like that, you realize that's all they are: details. What happened to my marriage wasn't about the last months of our time together and who did what, but the more basic fact that we were not truly compatible. I had spent thirteen years with this person. I had aligned my views of the world, friends, and hobbies with his. But I realized that I had compromised on too many things that were important to me—things I thought he would be able to change. But you can't base a healthy relationship on what you hope a person will become someday. It is not a given that they will grow and develop into the human being that is most compatible with you.

Suddenly I was all alone, and the world looked different. Even though I was devastated and in shock, I had this amazing revelation that I could start over again. It felt like an opportunity.

SHORTLY AFTER THE SEPARATION, I went out to dinner with a friend who helped me write down a list of what I needed in a man. Or maybe I should call it a list of what I could no longer compromise on. It would become my manifesto as I searched for a new partner. I knew my worth and I knew I was an exceptionally qualified partner for some amazing person out there. And I was going to find him. Using my "list of things I could no longer compromise on" as my guide, I swiped and swiped and swiped through dating apps. I swiped like my life depended on it.

I also meditated like my life depended on it. It was difficult at first. The breakup had been so sudden that I had a hard time closing my eyes and not remembering that horrible day. My TM teacher came to my rescue and left me a voicemail of a meditation prompt. It was a minute or so of her just guiding me back into the meditation practice. She said to only use it once and then delete it. And it worked. Once I could finally close my eyes for twenty minutes at a time and practice moments of peace, I think that really helped me heal quickly and move on successfully. But I knew it was an ongoing practice and that I would need to do it every day.

What really got me through that time was the support of all the people around me. From the first day of the breakup, I was very open with friends about what had happened. I knew that I needed their support to get me through this difficult life transition. In opening up to anyone and everyone I met in that next year about my recent divorce, I heard many stories from people who had gone through similar situations. I had never felt so connected to other people before. The perfectionist side of me, who had always operated as though sad moments in life had nothing to do with me, came off her pedestal and joined the rest of the universe by sharing painful feelings with others. As a result, I didn't feel alone.

In the end, my app-swiping worked. I went on a couple of dates, but one man in particular stood out. Oddly enough, he ended up checking every box I had on my list. And now we've been together for six years, gotten married, and started a family. I've kept my little list today as a reminder about the importance of manifesting what you want to come true, and not compromising on what you know you need in a partner.

For those of you young dancers out there who are just starting to date, please don't limit yourself to the ballet industry. There are so many wonderful people outside of the dance world who can bring color and texture to your life. Ballet is such an intense environment, and it's easy for your fellow students or company members to become your main social group. But if I could go back and do anything differently, I would try to expand my friendships outside of the company from an earlier age. It's a scary thing to do, especially when living in a big city like New York, but if you can find one good friend outside of your theater, that could lead to another of their friends, and so on. The more people you meet, the easier it is to surround yourself with people who are really right for you.

And that advice goes for people outside of the dance industry, too. Don't make your coworkers the only people you know. Diversify your friends, learn from people who are different from you. Be brave enough to venture outside of your comfort zone.

I'M SURE SOME PEOPLE are cringing when I use the word "failure." Most of us like to avoid it. It's usually such a negative word. But through my divorce, I've learned to embrace it. It was the biggest challenge that ever came my way, and I survived. Not only that, but I found out how strong and adaptable I was. And I learned a lot of lessons about how I wanted and needed to be living my life.

Success is a high, and we don't often need help from others to get us through it. But failure is a surprising opportunity for us to connect and come together in this amazing way, as well as to open our minds up to other possibilities and futures. So why do we always see these moments as negative? Maybe instead, we can start looking at failure as a wonderful learning opportunity and then stop being so afraid of it.

Success is a high, and we don't often need help from others to get us through it. But failure is a surprising opportunity for us to connect and come together in this amazing way, as well as to open our minds up to other possibilities and futures.

When I had that glimmer of hope at the end of my marriage—a possible life I hadn't yet imagined—I surprised myself with my ability to embrace the change. The direction I had been heading was obviously the wrong one. I never imagined that one day my marriage would end, and yet when it did, it was like I woke up from the little fairy tale I was living and was able to see my life really clearly.

I'd like to propose rerouting our thinking to see failure as an opportunity. I'm not saying that you should go searching for it, but rather that when something doesn't happen as you hoped it would—be it little or big—you use it as an opportunity for growth. We can learn from our mistakes and adjust our perspectives.

Failure of any kind can become a moment to start over. We get to reassess. We get to take stock of our lives and realize what does and doesn't matter to us. When you achieve success after success, you aren't going to look at your life and edit out the things that are wrong. You are going to keep plowing ahead. But a moment of failure is like a beautiful wakeup call—a whisper that maybe you need something different, something you'd never thought about.

That man who checked off all the boxes on my list was never going to enter my life if I hadn't gone through all the steps I went through. I know with certainty we would have never randomly crossed paths otherwise. I understand now that life upheavals, which feel like failures when you are in the thick of them, are just reroutes to finding the real path you are supposed to be on. I feel a lot truer to myself in my current relationship, and I am so grateful for the opportunity to start over again. And grateful I let the universe guide me in the right direction, however painful it was.

> *I understand now that life upheavals, which feel like failures when you are in the thick of them, are just reroutes to finding the real path you are supposed to be on.*

The perfectionist in me is not gone. I fight her expectations every day. But I have to remind myself of the grace I experienced in my moment of crisis, and also remind myself to continue to provide that kind of empathy for others when they are going through a hard time. I'm no longer naive enough to think that you can just will something to happen. We are not in control of many things in our lives, and embracing the unknown and the possibility of failure is incredibly freeing.

DIVERSIFYING
YOUR LIFE

∞

*Should you add other
commitments to your life,
or focus all your energy
on one thing?*

Ballet dancers start their careers earlier than those in other professions. As a senior in high school, I was already an apprentice with NYCB. Usually, dancers are happy just to graduate from high school, as it's difficult enough to juggle the schedule of a professional company with the last year or two of high school, let alone college. But I had always really enjoyed school, and since Fordham's Lincoln Center campus was right across the street from our theater, offering Monday evening classes, attending college was a possibility for me. I enrolled in my first class the fall of my first year out of high school, as a newly christened corps de ballet member.

I enjoyed my English class with Mr. Wasserman every Monday night, but when it got to writing my final paper, the stress of juggling the fifty shows of *Nutcracker* and a school deadline was too much for me to handle. I accomplished everything, but not without a whole lot of stress, and probably some tears in phone calls to my parents. After that experience, I thought it was just way too much to do dance and go to college, and I put my focus 100 percent back into the ballet.

Two years later, I tried again. By then I was a soloist with a lot of extra time on my hands while I waited for repertoire to come my way. When I did have rehearsal, it was always just me and a partner. The days were suddenly very lonely, and I felt isolated from the rest of my colleagues. Each week, when casting was posted, I hoped for something new or exciting to work toward. I wanted to learn and grow and be challenged, but I didn't always get the opportunity to do so. While I had spent a lot of my early career being pushed extremely quickly into difficult roles, there were also seasons that were very dry, and trying to find balance between those two extremes was difficult. It got to a point that was very demoralizing. My mom reminded me that I really enjoyed school, and if I had something else to work on while I was in a performance season, it would take a lot of pressure off casting. If I got cast in something—great! If not, then I would have extra energy to put into school. So we turned it into a win-win situation for me.

However, once again I found class to be too stressful to manage along with my new responsibilities at work. When I was given something special to perform, I wanted to make the most of it, and I still felt that taking a school class on the side was stretching myself too thin. I never like feeling that I can't give my all to my endeavors. So yet again, I put school aside for a while.

By the time I was an established principal, though, I had come to terms with my responsibilities at work and was learning how to handle the stress, so I enrolled in one of the required theology courses at Fordham. Every Monday night, I got to escape life and enter into this little academic bubble, where we discussed the universe and the usual existential questions. Coming from Utah, where everyone but me was the same religion, I found it incredibly refreshing to hear so many different, equally supported points of view. I started to see the value in group discussions guided by the professor, and I felt so refreshed and inspired by these weekly meetings.

School became a way to keep myself balanced in the incredibly intense and small world of ballet. Inside that theater where we spend our whole lives, everything we are doing seems like life or death. We are striving toward perfection, and we take our jobs incredibly serious. I needed a way to take the stress level down a notch. Once I was ready for the extra commitment of school, spending just three hours a week in another building where I was forced to focus on something other than ballet was a huge outlet for me. It was my way to take a step back and gain some perspective. I found it incredibly refreshing to flesh out another part of my life besides the ballet. To use my brain instead of my body. To have an opportunity to see myself not just as a dancer, and maybe stop taking myself so seriously. Returning to the theater after a school class, I always felt like I was seeing everything differently.

Needless to say, after this theology class that opened my eyes to the value of group learning and in-class discussions, I was hooked. I knew that school, especially in-class courses, was going to add a lot to my life and overall happiness. I was old enough to be able to juggle work and school. It fueled me and gave me energy, as opposed to taking it away as it did before. It's not always the right time to add more into our lives, but it is important not to get so settled in our ways that we never try to expand ourselves, our talents, and our brains. I can't say there is a recipe for when it *is* the right time, only that we need to be open-minded to that possibility as we move along, and try to feel out when we have that extra mental space to embrace something new. I'm so glad I kept knocking on that door and trying to commit. Eventually, the timing was right, and I was ready to pursue school as much as possible.

The next semester I registered for two classes and never really looked back. As I already had a full-time job, I never felt pressured to graduate within a certain time frame. My biggest goal was always to graduate by the time I was done dancing, which as a principal is usually anywhere from thirty-five to forty-five years old. If there was a semester that was extra busy with tours and such, I just took one class. Other times, two fit well. Sometimes I even took a leave of absence from school completely—once to plan my wedding, another time to go on Broadway. But most of the time I was usually taking at least one school class, often two. Every once in a while, school would conflict with rehearsal, and I would have to skip class and catch up later. It didn't always make sense to juggle both, but because school was giving me so much balance, and therefore happiness, it was a worthwhile endeavor.

Eventually, fifteen years after my first English class, I graduated, summa cum laude, with a major in economics and math.

Math had always been my favorite subject. I had no idea what I would ever do with it, but I wanted to study it because it came easily to me and I enjoyed it. I had reasoned initially that I had no idea where ballet would lead me, either; I just did it because I loved it, and so I would study math with the same lack of expectation. Just enjoying the process.

Math was an easy fit for ballet, or at least I believed so, because I could work on short math problems in between rehearsals. It is much easier to stop and start math homework than it is to stop and start reading a textbook or writing a paper. The thought process has to start from scratch, and you often find you have to re-read a lot of material. But a math problem, or even a couple of problems, can be accomplished in a short break, and so for years my dressing room was just an everlasting math problem. My textbooks were always open on my dressing-room spot, in between hair pins and stage makeup. Sterling Hyltin, my patient dressing-room mate, knew not to bother me if she came in when my head was down in my notebook.

Fifteen years is a long time to work toward a goal. At first, when I realized how long it took me to finish my undergrad, I was embarrassed. I thought that it seemed ridiculous and maybe even a little pathetic. But then I had to remind myself why I took so long. I had an amazing career going on throughout all of that, and to graduate at all was a huge accomplishment. If you had told me from the beginning that it would take me that long, I might have never started. But I just chipped away at it slowly, enjoying the journey and not waiting for the result. Because I didn't need the degree for my job, the act of going to school was a hobby for me. It engaged my mind in a way that stimulated me and brought me energy. It wasn't so much for the diploma at the end as it was to keep my mind healthy and entertained. I did it because it added fullness to my life.

However, I am at heart a planner. Since I was a child, I have loved making to-do lists in the morning and crossing things off as I completed them. I even have a ridiculous list that my mom saved, written on Hello Kitty paper, of my schedule as a nine-year-old. The first item of the day was "wake up." Then five minutes later "go downstairs." It included other tasks such as thirty minutes for reading, some other time for homework, practicing dances, and doing some abs! Looking back, it makes me laugh.

So while I wasn't going to school because I needed a diploma immediately, I did love that it was helping me work toward something I might do in the future after ballet. I was never content with letting ballet be the only thing in my life. I always wanted even more to look forward to. While I had never truly defined what that next step would be for me, I knew that getting a college degree would give me a lot more options!

Once I graduated, I was a little stumped about what to do next. My second husband, who knew my love of math and school and general life ambition, suggested I might really enjoy and get something out of getting an MBA. As a dancer, going to grad school—especially for something like an MBA—seemed incredibly intimidating and out of reach. I started the motions, however, replacing math homework with studying for the GMAT (the standardized test to apply for any business school). That summer, when my company was on tour in Saratoga Springs, I woke up a couple of hours earlier than the rest of my housemates to study my GMAT flashcards and take practice tests. I had bought all of the recommended study books, and the type-A in me was very satisfied about crossing off all of the recommended practice problems and study guides. But my first three practice tests saw little improvement. I totally panicked. I decided that I wasn't smart enough for business school and put the books aside for what I thought might be forever.

A couple of weeks later I got a second wind and reached out to a private tutor. Seeking help was the best money I ever spent. My tutor was able to quickly look over my practice tests and figure out which problems I was consistently missing. He also taught me some simple tricks for taking the GMAT. The stressful part about the test isn't that the questions are so hard, it's that sometimes if you don't know a quick trick, they can take forever. You technically only have two minutes for every problem, and that two minutes goes by incredibly fast. So he gave me skills to recognize similar styles of problems, and fast ways to approach them and find a quick answer.

Together, we decided on a goal test score that was appropriate to get me into the schools that I was interested in. Once my practice tests looked to be within that range, I went for the real deal. I was a ball of stress the day of the exam. I arrived so early at the test location, I had to spend an hour at a Starbucks across the street killing time. I was trying to keep my mind free and just stay relaxed, but that was easier said than done. The exam is just over three hours long and it is a real test of mental stamina. I remember the first couple of questions seemed to be unrecognizable, totally out of left field from practice problems I had been working on. It's possible they weren't, and I was just incredibly nervous and not able to think straight. But at any rate, just like I had the impulse to run off stage during my first performance as the Sugar Plum Fairy, three questions into the GMAT I thought about just grabbing my bag and going home. I was terrified. Then I finally landed on a question that was similar in style to the ones I had practiced with my tutor, and my confidence started to build. Somehow, I made it through the test.

After the last GMAT question, your score pops up immediately. It almost takes your breath away because you aren't ready to process it yet. I couldn't believe it. My score was higher than my goal, and I wouldn't ever have to take the test again!!! That night at home, I felt the way I do after performing a really hard ballet. All of the hard work, stress, worry, and fear turn into an elated adrenaline high. Like a performance, you have to commit to the prep work and hope that it will pay off in the end. And when it does, that is the greatest reward!

So now I'm back in school, this time business school at NYU Stern, and I am dealing with the balancing act of ballet and school all over again. This time is a little more difficult because I have started a family, and school isn't right across the street from my job like it was at Fordham. But it's still worth it to me.

The way I juggle it all now is by making the most of the time that my kids are at daycare. If you have kids yourself, you know that keeping your mind focused and accomplishing anything that requires a good attention span is impossible when they always need something from you. And I like to maximize every minute I have with my daughters. So instead of using down time in between class, rehearsals, or performances to chat with friends or go shopping nearby, the way I used to do before becoming a mom, I devote that time to my MBA homework. That way, no time is wasted, and on days when I don't have performances in the evening, I can pick my kids up and know that we have the rest of the day to ourselves.

I think a lot of people see outside commitments like school as possible distractions from their main focus. But for me, it has been what has allowed me to succeed in my job. Having something worthwhile to work on outside of the ballet studio took a ton of pressure off my career. The stress of being cast, the stress of performing as well as you know you can . . . Once I diversified my efforts in life, I started to dance even better. I wasn't clinging so tightly to this one main goal.

> *Having something worthwhile to work on outside of the ballet studio took a ton of pressure off my career.*

This also meant that I had many things that could bring me satisfaction and pride. If I only had ballet and I had a show that didn't go well, or I wasn't being cast much, I know I would have gone into a downward spiral that would have only made it more difficult for me to succeed. But taking my foot off the gas pedal a little bit and allowing myself to put energy into something else kept me from being constantly hung up on ballet, which paradoxically made my dancing even better.

RESTING AND
TAKING TIME OFF

❧

*How can you come back even
stronger after taking time away?*

Taking breaks as a dancer is always a bit scary. Even when you are burned out and exhausted, after about a week of rest, you'll quickly be raring to go again. Your body gets addicted to the exercise and your mind craves the peace that expression through movement can give you. And, to be honest, you also don't want to lose everything you've worked toward. Dancers work for hours each day to hone every body part, creating muscle memory and strength so that when we step out onto the stage and perform live for the audience, our body responds as we hope and command.

So many dancers dread taking an extended break. For those of you who aren't dancers, imagine spending weeks or months on a project and then forgetting to save the file on your computer and losing all of your work. That's what happens to a dancer's body when they take time off. We go from being highly conditioned athletes to regular people, and if too much time passes, we have to start all over again with our training.

In addition, there is a fear that we will lose some of our technique. To the non-dancer, I would explain technique as the way you organize and initiate movement in the body. It isn't enough to just pick your leg up and put it in a passé position, with your toe at your other knee. For a proper passé you must first shift your weight to your standing leg so that you can pull your working toes (the toes of the leg you're lifting) backward and your heel forward as you come to a beautiful coupé. And then, as you pull your leg higher to a full passé at the knee, that working heel should continue to push forward as that same knee pulls back and to the side.

For a pirouette, or a turn in passé, you don't just bounce up from a plié and spin around for a couple of turns. It all starts with a beautiful plié in fifth position. Don't let the front foot slip out to third position in an effort to find force for the turn. Don't let the back hip stick out in order to get a deeper (but artificial) plié. Then, from this perfect plié with equal weight on each foot, you push from the bottom to transfer your weight properly onto what will be your standing leg. During your beautiful journey to passé (described above), you must keep your hips and shoulders square as you take force from the arm of the standing leg to help bring yourself around. The hip in passé must be down, with your upper thigh rotated correctly so that it sits easily in your hip socket. Common errors include not keeping the passé turned out enough, probably due to a tilted pelvis; letting the front foot of the fifth position slip out at the end of the plié and allowing all of your weight to then fall away from the standing leg as you go for the turn; and not coordinating the arms with the legs.

These instructions cover only two short steps, so imagine all the work going on inside a dancer's head for a whole ballet! Every body part has a specific path it should take as you move from one ballet position to another. Slipping outside of these paths is what we consider bad technique.

It's like learning how to properly dice an onion. There is a wrong and a right way to approach it. The right way is efficient: it keeps the tip of the knife down so you have less of a chance of cutting your fingers, is faster and cleaner, and most of all, looks professional. The wrong technique of picking the knife up off the cutting board for every cut puts your fingers at risk of being chopped and results in pieces that aren't uniform.

Switching back from onions to dancers, perfect technique gives us a similar precision and efficiency of movement so we can move even faster. And, like the onion analogy, it keeps us safe. A sickled foot is the way most dancers sprain their ankles, so keeping perfect technique in mind is akin to keeping that tip of the knife down to avoid injury. And ultimately, the final outcome looks professional. It is what sets our dancing apart from an amateur's.

In 2010, I pushed taking a break a little too far. I took three or four weeks off after a spring season at NYCB to get married and take a honeymoon before performing a gig in Sicily. If there was ever a good excuse for letting go a little bit, this seemed like it! But squeezing real life into a ballet dancer's year can sometimes be really difficult. We can't just take vacations wherever we want because to be in proper dancing shape, we need a studio with plenty of space, a ballet barre, and a sprung floor with a Marley dance floor on top. Well, at our Saint Lucia honeymoon resort, there was no proper dancing floor—it's not exactly a common resort amenity— and the honeymoon was going to cut into my precious prep time for the gig. I would have only three days upon my return to New York City to prepare for it. I knew I would have to really buckle down and focus during those three days, but I thought it would be fine. My muscles would remember.

Wasn't I sorry! I don't think I have ever been so sore, or performed so sore, in all my life. The ballet I was tasked with on this gig was *Tarantella* (the dancer equivalent of running a marathon) and a variation in *Who Cares?*, and boy, were my calves screaming at me. My first day back in the studio, I gave myself a proper ballet barre and center, and then just ran the ballet all the way through. What better way to get into shape than one of the more stamina-pushing ballets?

Yes, my muscles did remember what to do, but inside, my body was working overtime to keep up. And the next day, when I could barely walk, I had to get up and push my body again!

I was suffering from extreme soreness, caused by lactic acid in the muscles. When you need intense bursts of energy (especially when you haven't built up the stamina), your muscles convert to anaerobic respiration, and the byproduct is lactic acid in the muscles. Just touching my calves hurt. I had no choice, though, but to push through that pain and keep working to make up for lost time. The shows went fine, but I was in too much pain to enjoy the experience of dancing outside on a stage in Palermo, a city on the northwest coast of Sicily. It was an amazing experience, but what I remember most was my regret about not training for the gig earlier.

I was hoping that just once, I could enjoy my beautiful beach vacation and not have ballet on the to-do list for the day. Unfortunately, I had to learn the hard way that there are no shortcuts when it comes to what we do. You are either ready and primed to perform, or you aren't. And when you aren't, you will be in a lot of pain and you may hurt yourself. Needless to say, I never gave myself this little prep time ever again!

WHEN I GOT THE OPPORTUNITY to take a leave of absence from the ballet and go to Broadway for a year, I knew the biggest concern from my boss would be that I might lose my grip on my technique. It was a hallmark of my dancing, something that made me stand out from the rest, and by taking a year away from rigorous ballet training, I was risking my exceptionality. But by this time I was thirty years old and I knew how and why certain steps worked for me. I could self-correct and adjust to maintain consistency in the hardest of ballets, and this knowledge was the reason that it felt safe to leave.

While no one ever knows when they sign a Broadway contract how long the run will actually last, this show was a success, and it ended up running a little over a year. Because of the grueling nature of a Broadway show, I had not trained seriously in ballet for the entire year. I knew I would have to retrain my body completely to get back to the ballet in proper shape. During my last couple of months in *On the Town,* when the SAB summer course began, I attended classes every day like I was one of the students, while performing in my Broadway show at night. The entire class was on pointe, and I suddenly felt my muscles changing back to the body I once had. I was surprised to feel my thigh muscles lengthen in a different way from the way they had evolved from dancing in three-inch heels for a year, and it was so refreshing to start to get my "ballet body" back!

After Broadway I realized that the ballet world was where I belonged. It was a relief to return to my comfort zone and the style of dance I was best at after a year of stretching my abilities and playing a sexy role in high heels. Putting the pointe shoes back on was like returning home, and it was so nice to settle back into something where I could be completely confident in my talent.

Another thing I had learned while doing Broadway was that just me was enough. I had spent most of my time in the ballet world trying to fit into the mold of perfect ballerina. Corrections are constant and you are always expected to analyze your dancing and improve, whether artistically or technically. On Broadway, on the other hand, I rarely received any feedback from the director or choreographer about my approach to the role. I was always waiting for them to sit me down and say something like, "The character is really more like this, so we need you to do x, y, and z better," but they never did. Slowly I realized that they liked me exactly as I was—they trusted my instincts as an actor. It was a revelation to feel like just me was enough. I had never experienced that feeling before in the ballet world, where everything could always be better.

Living for a year with the "just me is enough" mentality was incredibly liberating. It really educated me as a performer, as did the education of how audiences respond to the same show in different ways night after night. I learned to trust in my instincts, feel comfortable in my skin, and sell the show!

Upon returning to the ballet, these new skills and realizations proved career-changing. I was hungry to get back to ballet. As a ballerina, I felt more sure of myself than ever, and I was able to really embrace the diva confidence I had always been searching for. People started to comment that I came back even better, and I just felt pure freedom out on stage. It was enjoyable for me finally. No longer was I starting each performance saying, "It's almost over." I was truly cherishing every moment on that stage dancing to that enormous live orchestra we are so blessed with at the ballet.

While this break away from the ballet world wasn't necessarily rest, as I was dancing and singing on Broadway every night for a year, it was *space* from the ballet world. Without that space and change of scenery, I never would have learned the life lessons I did. I had been given this wonderful gift of perspective outside of the ballet bubble, which helped me better understand my place as an artist.

A COUPLE OF YEARS LATER, post-divorce and post-Broadway, my new partner and I decided to start a family. People often think that when dancers have babies, it's the beginning of the end—the point when they start slowing down in their careers. But for me, stepping away from the stage to take maternity leave made me want to get back to it even more, just like after Broadway. By the time I started training again, six weeks postpartum, my body had developed a hunger to move like never before. I am petite and I had a large baby—over eight pounds—so toward the end I was really immobile compared to my usual lifestyle as a dancer. Just getting up from bed or off the couch was a difficult move for me during those last couple of months of pregnancy.

The first weeks after my C-section, I made sure to walk every day to avoid blood clots. This turned into a habit of walking for forty-five minutes with the stroller each day. After six weeks, I was cleared to really exercise, so I returned to the pool that had gotten me through most of my pregnancy. I thought that I would maybe swim a lap and do a baby ballet barre before going home. But then

I got in the water and didn't get out for an hour. I swam twenty laps followed by a ballet barre in the water at the side of the pool for the next three weeks straight. My body was so thirsty to move again, and the freedom of no longer carrying another human in me was exhilarating.

I enjoyed my post-pregnancy training immensely. It was like a weird experiment to see the body transform so much. Like chipping away at a block of undefined stone to create a beautiful statue. I had gained a little over thirty pounds during my pregnancy, and now I was whittling away at my body, finding my muscles again and seeing my posture return to normal. It was oddly fun for me, and I liked the challenge. I'm sure that's one of the reasons I have had success as a ballet dancer: I like the behind-the-scenes parts almost as much as I do the performing. I like whipping my body into shape, I like the feeling I get after a good workout, and I like pushing myself mentally to do more than I think I can.

Pilates was what really helped me come back quickly. I would see my Pilates teacher twice a week for crazy two-hour sessions (they didn't even feel like work, it was just so nice to do everything again), and very quickly my body remembered what it did before. At five months postpartum, I was back onstage performing. Little did the audience know that under my thin leotard, I had my stomach taped together to hold the muscles back in proper alignment. I had developed a four-finger-wide separation between my rectus abdominis muscle (the midline of my six-pack muscles), also known as diastasis recti, during pregnancy. My OB had put me in touch with an amazing diastasis recti physical therapist, and she put me in a brace that I wore day and night for months and taught me exercises to repair my muscles. They never quite returned to normal, but they got pretty dang close.

My arabesque took the longest to come back, probably because I was afraid to open the stomach muscles that I was so desperately working to bring back together. It took more than a year postpartum for it to return to normal.

What was most surprising to me was that after both these extended breaks—Broadway and having a baby—I came back to greater success. I truly think that those moments of stepping away made me so hungry to get back out there and reinhabit that feeling of being a ballerina that I became an even better dancer afterward.

Although it takes incredible dedication and commitment to become a great dancer, or a great anything, sometimes the daring act of stepping away, by choice, can make you even better than if you never left. It's like scrubbing dirty dishes. You can scrub and scrub and scrub, but sometimes, the dishes just need to soak overnight. Sometimes taking a step back is a good thing. You let the body and mind have a chance to casually absorb the information you are constantly trying to force feed it, and in doing so, have an opportunity to gain perspective, as your muscles have had time to repair. And if you give yourself enough time to retrain when you start up again, you can eventually pick up from where you left off. Most importantly, the mind is hungry to push and challenge you again.

> *Sometimes the daring act of stepping away, by choice, can make you even better than if you never left.*

I was always trying my best at the ballet, so it was very odd to me that I got such great results and feedback when I returned from extended time away. I must have learned something during my time off that added to my dancing and artistry upon returning. Allowing myself the freedom to have these life experiences away from the daily grind of ballet barres and intense scrutiny helped me become the artist I was meant to be. Finding my best dancing didn't happen in the studio. It happened when I stepped away and allowed myself to have deeper experiences outside of that world that I could then bring back and add to my dancing.

I think the moral of this story is that you have to make room for other life experiences in order to evolve enough as a human being to truly be your best in whatever you are pursuing. If we put our nose to the grindstone and never come up for air, we don't have the proper perspective or context to let the results of that hard work fully shine.

I SHOULD SAY THAT these times away from the company would have been different if I had been out of commission due to injury. My months away were life affirming and confidence building, and so I returned self-assured, rested, and happy. I stepped away by choice, and I came back by choice. I know this helped immensely in my successful return to the stage after each break. Coming back from an injury or other forced periods of rest, on the other hand, can be a big blow to your confidence, and you have to really be your own cheerleader the whole time to get through it. That can be exhausting.

During the coronavirus pandemic, dancers everywhere were forced to stop training. All the hard work everyone had been putting in to be in their best shape was lost, because we no longer had access to our precious studios with special ballet floors. The momentum completely came to a standstill and we all had to learn how to adapt.

Initially when the shutdown happened, I panicked, because I felt like I had to be able to return to the stage exactly as I had left it. But I soon realized I would have to let the engine cool down and breathe a bit by decreasing my training, and take it back up again later, when we were closer to returning. I knew I didn't have the willpower to maintain high morale from just dancing for a year and a half in my apartment, and when we got back to dancing, I didn't want to be burned-out from the experience. I also wanted to make sure I didn't get an injury. Dancing on my apartment floor, which has a cement subfloor, was not good for my aging dancer's body. So I let it go again, trusting that I would find it back on the other side.

I saw my entire industry frantically try to keep in shape in their confined spaces. While I did continue to train a little in the five-by-six-foot area of Marley I had at home, I also had these two valuable experiences of leaving my job and returning in the back of my mind. Twice before I had done the ballet equivalent of forgetting to save my file, losing all the work, and finding it back again each time on my own. Because of this, I wasn't worried for the final return—I knew I had already accomplished it twice before. I know that having this ability to let my grip on my dancing go during the pandemic was a real luxury that most dancers didn't feel they had.

I knew it was important to embrace the experience so I didn't feel like a victim to the shutdown. To adapt and find new things to work on. What could I do with this unexpected time? What did I want to show at the end of it: a new skill, a new hobby, a new relationship with my self and identity? Who was I, besides a ballet dancer? We work so hard from such a young age to be professional dancers that it can be disorienting when dance isn't a big part of our lives anymore. What was I supposed to do with myself?

> *I knew it was important to embrace the experience so I didn't feel like a victim.*

Being able to give myself a little room to take a step back and let go of all that work temporarily is a scary thing to do. But I have started to see that my best dancing happens when I am both physically and mentally healthy. In the book *The 5 Love Languages*, by Gary Chapman, there's an analogy that everyone has these "love tanks" that need to be filled in order to have a healthy relationship. (If you don't know this book, it's a must-read for understanding certain relationships!) I like to extend this analogy to my own health and well-being. Let's imagine you have these imaginary tanks, one for physical health and one for mental health, that both need refueling and maintenance. The goal is to have them both at their fullest when that opportunity for performance happens. And these two tanks are intertwined. When you're not feeling physically healthy and your physical tank is running low, it can be a strain on your mental health, and lower its levels. When your mental tank is low, it can be hard for you to push yourself physically and refuel the physical tank. Knowing they are intertwined and seeing that to be your best self, they both need to be filled, puts you one step closer to fulfilling your greatest potential.

Spending a year letting my physical tank drop down a bit gave my mental tank lasting fuel for my company's return to the stage. Leading up to our company's comeback, I knew when to start applying pressure to push my body into top athletic form. If I had pushed myself physically through the whole pandemic, with no actual output of performing that gives me the emotional reward for all of my hard work, I would have become incredibly burned-out.

Taking steps away from the work we care about can be scary, even when it's by choice. When it's not by choice, it can be even scarier. But if we approach our periods of rest in the right way, they can make us even better at our art. When we do finally have the opportunity to return, we'll be more inspired and well-rounded human beings with a better understanding of who we are outside of work.

A GREATER
GOAL

⸎

*What would you want if
you were able to achieve absolutely
everything in your career?*

When I was a young dancer in Utah dancing in the Ballet West *Nutcracker*, I found out one day that a former dancer with the company had committed suicide. I was so saddened to hear that she had not seen a life for herself worth living anymore. Ever since then, I've kept this very morbid but important notion in mind: "There has to be more to life after ballet."

This mindset stayed with me as I moved to New York and joined New York City Ballet. What seemed like incredible highs in life—getting promoted to soloist and then principal, dancing the hardest of ballets for packed audiences of almost three thousand people, hearing huge applause as a reward for all my hard work—had a flip side. I knew from the very beginning that those moments were ephemeral and fleeting. It depressed me to think that for many dancers, the highlight of their life is over at age thirty or forty or whenever they have to say goodbye to the stage.

When you find something that you are so passionate about, it can be devastating when you have to give it up someday, as all dancers eventually have to do. I have always tried to be aware that these dancing years could be the best time of my life if I wasn't careful, and that thought always motivated me to keep a greater goal than just ballet. Thanks to that early understanding that mental health after a ballet career can be precarious, I always tried to make sure that I was aiming further into my future, and not focusing only on the present and getting caught up in the excitement of what was directly in front of me.

Throughout my career I've seen many dancers saying goodbye to this profession we have worked so long and hard toward. Some did it incredibly gracefully, but some worried me. What did they have to go on to? What was left to inspire them outside of the walls of this theater? Could they handle suddenly not being the center of attention? These thoughts really consumed me.

As I became more established in my role as a principal in the company, I thought a lot about setting a greater goal. I was determined for my best years to not end at forty. I wanted to find something that would bring me more everlasting joy than just a well-received performance. I was determined to make my life bigger than my performing career. What was I going to do after ballet, and how was I going to make sure that I liked that life just as much as the one that was happening now?

One of the things I really didn't want was for my best money-making years to be over at age forty, when I retired from ballet.

That's why I went back to school to get my MBA—so that upon retirement, I could get a new job that was as fulfilling as it was financially fruitful.

But in addition, I didn't want my ballet career, which could last up to twenty-five years, to cause me to miss out on being a mom. For me, living my fullest life meant creating a family for myself. It's not true for everyone, but that's what I knew would make me feel satisfied at the end of my career. Having a family was even more important to me than lining up a second job.

I started to notice that a lot of the dancers who transitioned well had a family. This is not to say you can't happily retire from ballet if you don't have a life partner and a child, but for many dancers, starting a family was the way they chose to diversify their lives and prepare for the next chapter. I always felt so peaceful and proud when I watched a retiring dancer's kids come onto the stage as part of their entourage to give them a hug upon their final bow. It showed me that those dancers were definitely more than the four walls of the theater. They had these whole other lives I didn't even know about.

If you are a female principal dancer and you are blessed to have a long career, you run the risk of missing out on your fertile years. I knew from a very early age that I was going to have to take a step away from the stage here and there to start the family that I knew I always wanted. It would be a sacrifice, but I knew when the time was right, that it would be the best investment I could make in my future happiness. If I missed out on having a family, I would always feel bitter about my career, and I didn't want to feel that way. I was determined to find a balance between it all.

After my divorce at thirty-one, one of the many things that left me feeling devastated was that I suddenly felt late in my plans to have a family. Here I had thought everything was all laid out for me and "the plan" was in place: I had my person and my house, and when I felt old enough and ready, we would have kids. Having to start all over again put me in a panic. For someone like me, who feels safest when following a well-thought-out plan, this was a scary time of uncertainty.

Thankfully, I soon found an amazing new life partner, and our relationship continued to grow and blossom into something immensely greater than my previous marriage. Eventually I started getting the baby bug. Severely! I was so jealous of anyone who had a family already that I was soon unable to socialize with anyone who had kids without crying afterward, and I stopped following all of them on social media. For a couple of years, it felt that my life was on pause until I met my first-born. I was so sick of waiting. I wanted to meet them. I wanted to know what they looked like. I wanted a house with some chaos and noise. Everything felt too quiet.

Getting this baby fever made it easy to decide to take the plunge into starting a family and taking the inevitable step away from the stage. I was lucky enough to have spent fourteen years as a principal without ever having been sidelined for a major injury, and so in my mind, I was taking my "injury year." Most of my principal colleagues had taken a year for serious injury at some point in their career, and this maternity leave was mine.

My colleague Ashley Bouder, another female principal, already had a three-year-old, and she was a great example and resource for me as I prepared to take time away from ballet. She danced through most of her pregnancy. I took a different approach, as I just didn't feel comfortable jumping around with a baby in my belly. When I was sixteen weeks along, I took my last company class for that year. I took the extra time to travel to France and take a three-week language immersion course. My partner is French, and I was really focused on making sure our baby would be bilingual. Taking three weeks to do something like that is something I never would have otherwise felt I was able to do if I was still immersed in the rigors of the day-to-day life of a ballerina.

I continued to train while being pregnant as I knew this would be one of the greatest physical challenges I would ever put my body through. Thankfully we lived in a building with an outdoor pool, and as soon as I stopped taking ballet class, the pool opened up for the summer. A couple of times a week I would go downstairs, swim my twenty laps, do a little ballet barre at the side of the pool in the water, and then call it a day! I also took childbirth classes from a former NYCB dancer turned doula/yoga instructor/childbirth educator. After about fifteen hours of hearing how the labor process would go, I felt totally ready.

As a dancer, I could always make my body do whatever I

wanted it to do if I put my mind to it. I felt I had the tools to have the most natural delivery and breast-feeding experience. But my baby had different plans, and we finally brought our daughter into the world via C-section. It was a possibility I had tried to prepare myself for, but a week after her birth, I started to experience a lot of anger toward my body and toward other women who had been able to give birth naturally. For the first time in my life, I had not been able to command my body to do what I asked it to do.

I realized that my dancer-trained body was not superior. I was just like everyone else. Not in control. It was humbling as a professional dancer to come to that realization, and it also made me feel very connected to all the other women who have had to go through these scary, painful, and stressful moments to give birth. It was comforting and frustrating at the same time.

It took me almost a whole year to get over these feelings of frustration and inadequacy. But when I started to see other friends go through their own experiences of motherhood, each with their own blips and bumps along the road, I started to realize that the things I was obsessing over were just minor details. The only thing that mattered was that my baby and I were healthy and happy. Sure, people had been reminding me of this all along the way, but it took me a full year to really believe it. I was starting to learn that I was not perfect, and that no one should be. My intense, goal-oriented self finally learned to take a back seat and let the natural progression of life be my guide.

I think a lot of my success as a dancer comes from a certain stubbornness to work on something until I can get it right. You truly have to be stubborn to work as endlessly and as hard as we do. And I was now learning that sometimes I needed to give up my stubbornness and go with the flow. I always wished I could be one of those people who could just naturally roll with the punches, but now I was being forced to figure it out. It took a lot of time, and boy did I fight it along the way, but eventually I got there.

Of course, the best thing to come out of all of this was my daughter. I finally got to meet her and see what she looked like. She was my buddy and we loved to giggle together. I think the best thing about being a parent is seeing your child's eyes light up with wonderment about something. It's like you are experiencing the magic of the world with them for the very first time. Yes, there are hard moments, but it's worth it when they shout, "Mama!" at something they are excited about. Seeing them smile is like a shot of oxytocin.

When I did return to work, I truly loved dropping my daughter off at daycare and seeing her in a new setting, having social experiences outside the walls of our small apartment. She was having a great and full day, with new songs and lessons that I didn't know to teach her, and I could go back to doing my thing. The moments away from her were even sweeter because I was hell-bent on making the most of my time without her. So when I was at work I was making every class, every extra minute count. If I had time in between rehearsals I was in the Pilates room, or working on some homework, instead of just milling around waiting for rehearsal.

The value of my time changed. And then I enjoyed picking her up from daycare just as much as I had loved dropping her off. We had the best evenings together.

I still love what I do for a living. I felt bad about this at first, as though I should be wanting to spend all my time with my daughter. Once I asked my OB, who is always working at her office or in the hospital and who has three children, how she manages. I really looked up to her as someone who was able to fully enjoy both being at work without her kids and being home with them, without any guilt either way. She responded, "I love my kids and I love my job." Simple as that. And that's how I feel, too. No more guilt. Bringing a child into our lives only sweetened every moment.

No MATTER WHAT WE DO for a living, we are all more than our work. And as an artist, I am more than just my art. I am also more than just a mom. I don't feel I need to be completely defined by either title.

> *No matter what we do for a living,*
> *we are all more than our work.*

Being a mom has not taken away my focus from my career; it's made it more productive and fruitful. Since returning to the stage after having my daughter, I've danced in all these ballets I'd never been a part of before. I had a career renaissance, and I've enjoyed it. Work isn't this stressful thing anymore—it's the place I go to fulfill other sides of me besides the mom side.

Having a child has also put all of those exhausting moments of work at the theater into perspective. It's challenging to bring a child into the world and raise them. Sure, being a ballet dancer is hard, but it became the easiest part of my day. And I think that realization made me even better at my difficult job.

I think it's important not to assume that reaching the top in your career will bring you happiness forever. I certainly realized after I was promoted to principal that the promotion didn't solve all of my problems. What would you want if you were able to achieve absolutely everything in your career?

> *It's important not to assume that reaching the top in your career will bring you happiness forever.*

While my career has always been a top priority for me, there is something greater than dance. And in no way does it take away from my focus or commitment to my job. The cliché of the struggle of finding balance, the fear that having a family makes you less formidable in your work—well, I just know from personal experience that that's not true. Going after the things that I wanted in life, like having a family, made me a more fulfilled and content person in the studio and on the stage. And when you are an artist, that mental and emotional side of you matters. It affects the kind of performance you can give to the audience. When you feel full, you have more to give.

ACKNOWLEDGMENTS

I would have never written this book if it wasn't for Emily Neuberger, my first editor at Penguin, who used my advice from my *Ask Megan* podcast to help her run a marathon. Thank you, Emily, for your vision for what this book could be, and for helping me create something useful out of my experiences.

And for the podcast opportunity that led to this book, I must thank Kimberly Falker, my podcast producer. Thanks to you, Kimberly, I had enough confidence to start sharing my opinions on the best practices for young dancers and their parents trying to navigate the complicated and stressful industry of ballet.

My manager, Pamela Cooper, has helped me navigate my way through Cole Haan endorsements, Broadway, and now this book. Thanks for always protecting me and helping me dream big.

Gretchen Schmid, my second editor at Penguin, helped me find a clear voice on paper and reminded me what was universal in my stories.

For the balance I have found in life and many of the lessons I have learned along the way, I must thank my amazing parents.

ACKNOWLEDGMENTS

Having no previous knowledge of the ballet world, they have always been there to support me, whether it be physically or emotionally, and I credit them with my ability to keep a straight head in this competitive industry.

Thank you to Jen Turner for your last-minute read-through and insight in the eleventh hour.

Huge thank you to my husband for all of your support in my endeavors, pushing me to dream bigger than I would have ever thought possible. Your support during some of my biggest opportunities has helped me reach goals I would have never had the confidence to pursue on my own. And finally, thank you to my three beautiful daughters, who have shown me how big my heart can grow and given me great perspective on what's truly important in life.